EURIPIDES

in an hour

BY CARL R. MUELLER

SUSAN C. MOORE, SERIES EDITOR

PLAYWRIGHTS in an hour
know the playwright, love the play

IN AN HOUR BOOKS • HANOVER, NEW HAMPSHIRE • INANHOURBOOKS.COM
AN IMPRINT OF SMITH AND KRAUS PUBLISHERS, INC • SMITHANDKRAUS.COM

*With grateful thanks to Carl R. Mueller, whose
fascinating introductions to his translations of the
Greek and German playwrights provided
inspiration for this series.*

Published by In an Hour Books
an imprint of Smith and Kraus Publishers, Inc.
177 Lyme Road, Hanover, NH 03755
inanhourbooks.com SmithandKraus.com

Know the playwright, love the play.

In an Hour, In a Minute, and Theater IQ are registered trademarks
of In an Hour Books.

© 2009 by In an Hour Books
All rights reserved
Manufactured in the United States of America
First Edition: April 2010
10 9 8 7 6 5 4 3 2 1

All rights reserved including the right of reproduction in whole or in part
in any form except for use in reviews of the book and/or series. Please
direct inquiries to In an Hour Books (603) 643-6431.

All scenes are © 2005 by Carl R. Mueller. Reprinted by permission of Hugh
Denard, Executor of the estate of Carl R. Mueller. For performance rights, contact
Smith and Kraus, Inc., licensing@smithandkraus.com, smithandkraus.com.

Front cover design by Dan Mehling, dmehling@gmail.com
Text design by Kate Mueller, Electric Dragon Productions
Book production by Dede Cummings Design, DCDesign@sover.net

ISBN-13: 978-1-936232-11-6

ACC LIBRARY SERVICES AUSTIN, TX

CONTENTS

Why Playwrights in an Hour?

This new series by Smith and Kraus Publishers titled Playwrights in an Hour has a dual purpose for being: one academic, the other general. For the general reader, this volume, as well as the many others in the series, offers in compact form the information needed for a basic understanding and appreciation of the works of each volume's featured playwright. Which is not to say that there don't exist volumes on end devoted to each playwright under consideration. But inasmuch as few are blessed with enough time to read the splendid scholarship that is available, a brief, highly focused accounting of the playwright's life and work is in order. The central feature of the series, a thirty- to forty-page essay, integrates the playwright into the context of his or her time and place. The volumes, though written to high standards of academic integrity, are accessible in style and approach to the general reader as well as to the student and, of course, to the theater professional and theatergoer. These books will serve for the brushing up of one's knowledge of a playwright's career, to the benefit of theater work or theatergoing. The Playwrights in an Hour series represents all periods of Western theater: Aeschylus to Shakespeare to Wedekind to Ibsen to Williams to Beckett, and on to the great contemporary playwrights who continue to offer joy and enlightenment to a grateful world.

Carl R. Mueller
School of Theater, Film and Television
Department of Theater
University of California, Los Angeles

Introduction

Although his last plays were performed at the end of the fifth century BCE, the ancient Greek dramatist Euripides may very well be remembered as the grandfather of modern Western drama. Henrik Ibsen is often credited with having invented contemporary realism, but it was actually Euripides who first explored the possibilities of that form.

While Aeschylus and Sophocles — along with all those forgotten Attic dramatists whose plays exist only in shards and fragments — were piously exploring the relationship between humans and the gods, Euripides — or at least some of his characters — was expressing a surprising skepticism. Although Euripides makes greater use of the deus ex machina — where a god materializes onstage to resolve the plot — than any of his contemporaries, often his heroes are either unhappy with the Olympian deities ("I am angry against the gods," says the chorus in *Hippolytus)* or refuse to believe in their existence. And this religious skepticism, coupled with Euripides' psychological insights, feminist concerns, and pacifist beliefs (his anti-war tirades are among the most passionate in literature) mark him as a man born well before his time. Years ago, Jan Kott wrote a book called *Shakespeare Our Contemporary. Euripides Our Contemporary* could very well be the prequel.

Euripides' heretical qualities occasionally marked him as an object of satire and of scorn. The comic and more conservative dramatist Aristophanes delighted in making fun of Euripides, particularly his lightweight writing style, his disrespect for the gods, and his attitude toward women. In *Women at the Thesmophoria*, for example, Aristophanes characterized Euripides as a misogynist, who portrays women either as mad, murderous, or extremely lustful.

The irony is that Euripides created the most complicated female characters in Greek drama, and often the most sympathetic ones. It is true that Medea gets her revenge on a faithless husband by killing all of their children, and it is also true that many of Euripides' other heroines refuse to conform to traditional female roles. But even pious Aeschylus created an extremely malignant heroine — Clytemnestra who competes with Medea as one of the most murderous females in dramatic literature.

Nor should we forget that it was Euripides — that passionate poet of peace — who depicted the female sex, in that most sublime of anti-war plays, *Trojan Women,* as the suffering victims of male bellicosity. Ironically, the only poet who matches the power of Euripides' pacifism is his archenemy, Aristophanes, who imagined women, in *Lysistrata,* putting an end to the Peloponnesian Wars, simply by refusing to submit to the sexual demands of their husbands.

Euripides was certainly a religious skeptic, possibly even an atheist. But he also believed that denying the existence of the power of specific gods would inevitably lead to catastrophe. In *Bacchae,* for example, the resistance of King Pentheus to the ecstatic new religion of the half-god Dionysus results in that unbeliever's death at the hands of his own mother (thinking him a lion, she tears off his head). Here the rationalist Euripides, however reluctantly, affirms the overwhelming power of Dionysus, as embodied in his orgiastic followers.

In *The Birth of Tragedy,* the nineteenth-century German philosopher Frederick Nietzsche made much the same point, writing that the Dionysian element in Greek drama — the spirit of ecstasy, drunkenness, and abandonment — was its animating feature. But Nietzsche further believed that these qualities were in danger of being displaced by the empty rationalism invented by Socrates, and imported by Euripides, "the poet of aesthetic Socratism," into Attic drama. It is true that Euripides introduced a much more realistic element into Greek tragedy, creating a form that, sometimes resembling tragicomedy, would later lead to the domesticated comedies of Menander. His ordered rationalism may explain why he became such an important influence on the French classical writers (particularly on Racine who adapted his Hippolytus into a superior play called *Phèdre).*

But like all great artists, Euripides manages to escape all attempts to categorize him. He stands with one foot firmly planted on the solid soil of fifth-century Greece — and the other teetering on our own more treacherous terrain.

Robert Brustein
Founding Director of the Yale and American Repertory Theatres
Distinguishing Scholar in Residence, Suffolk University
Senior Research Fellow, Harvard University

Euripides

IN A MINUTE

AGE YEAR (BCE)

AGE	YEAR	
—	480	Enter Euripides (born in the 480s, exact birth date unknown).
1	479	The Battle of Plataea routs Persian invaders from Greece.
4	476	Phrynichus — *Phoenissae*
8	472	Aeschylus — *The Persians*
9	471	Tribunes in Rome are first elected by plebian assembly.
12	468	Sophocles defeats Aeschylus, winning first prize at the Dionysia.
16	464	A series of devastating earthquakes hit Sparta.
19	461	Pericles assumes leadership at Athens, ushering in the Athenian Golden Age.
22	458	Aeschylus — *The Oresteia*
25	455	**Euripides — *Daughters of Pelias***
30	450	Roman law codified in twelve tables.
31	449	The Greeks sign a peace treaty with the Persian ruler Artaxerxes I.
35	445	Persian emperor Artaxerxes I permits Nehemiah to return as governor to Jerusalem and to rebuild it.
37	443–442	Sophocles — *Antigone* (date uncertain)
39	**441**	**Euripides wins his first victory at the City Dionysia (play unknown).**
49	431	The Second Peloponnesian War begins, pitting Athens against Sparta for Greek hegemony.
50	**430**	**Euripides — *Children of Heracles***
56	424	Socrates reportedly saves Alcibiades' life at the Battle of Delium.
57	**423**	**Euripides — *The Suppliant Women***
58	422	Aristophanes — *The Wasps*
59	421	The Peace of Nicias between Athens and Sparta.
60	420	Bellicose Alcibiades is elected *strategos* (military leader).
65	**415**	**Euripides — *The Trojan Women***
66	414	Aristophanes — *The Birds*
67	**413**	**Euripides — *Electra***
68	**412**	**Euripides — *Helen***
69	411	Coup d'etat in Athens; power transferred to the people's assembly.
70	**c. 410**	**Euripides — *Phoenician Women***
74	**406**	**Exit Euripides**.
—	405	**Euripides — *The Bacchae* and *Iphigenia at Aulis* (produced posthumously)**

In one minute or less, this section gives you a snapshot of the playwright's world. From historical events to the literary landscape of the time, this brief list catalogues events that directly or indirectly impacted the playwright's writing.

Euripides

HIS WORKS

All caps indicate an existing play.

DRAMATIC WORKS
Dates Known

Alcmaeon in Psophis [438]

ALCESTIS [438]

Alexandrus [415]

ANDROMACHE [c. 425]

Andromeda [412]

BACCHAE [after 406]

CHILDREN OF HERACLES [430]

Cretan Women [438]

CYCLOPS (date uncertain)

Daughters of Pelias [455]

Dictys [431]

ELECTRA [c. 420]

HECUBA [424]

HELEN [412]

HIPPOLYTUS [428]

ION [c. 413]

IPHIGENIA IN AULIS [after 406]

IPHIGENIA IN TAURIS [c. 414]

THE MADNESS OF HERACLES [c. 416]

MEDEA [431]

ORESTES [408]

Palamedes [415]

This section presents a complete list of the playwright's works.

Dates Unknown

Onstage with Euripides

*Introducing Colleagues and
Contemporaries of Euripides*

 THEATER

Aeschylus, Athenian tragic playwright [525–456]

Aristophanes, Athenian comic playwright [448–380]

Crates, Athenian Old Comedy playwright [mid-5th c.]

Cratinus, Athenian Old Comedy playwright [520–423]

Epicharmus, Sicilian Greek comic poet, [ca. 540–450]

Phrynichus, Greek tragic playwright [511–476]

Pratinas, introduced satyr play to Athens [late 6th–early 5th c.]

Sophocles, Athenian tragic playwright [496–406]

Sophron, Syracusan writer of mimes [ca. 5th c.]

 ARTS

Micon, Greek painter [mid-5th c.]

Phidias, Greek sculptor [ca. 480–ca. 430]

Polyclitus, Greek sculptor [450–420]

Polygnotus, Greek painter [500–440]

 POLITICS/MILITARY

Agesilaus II, king of Sparta [444–360]

Alcibiades, Athenian general and politician [ca. 450–404]

Aristides, founded Delian League [530–468]

Artaxerxes, king of Persia [ca. 5th c.]

Cimon of Athens, Athenian statesman [510–450]

Cyrus the Younger, Persian prince and general, [ca. 5th c.]

Darius II, king of Persia [ca. 5th c.–404]

Herodotus, Greek historian [ca. 484–ca. 425]

This section lists contemporaries whom the playwright may or may not have known. Since fewer notables are known from the Classical Period, we have included some who predated the playwright.

Mardonius, Persian military commander [ca. 5th c.–479]
Nicias, Athenian statesman and general [469–413]
Pericles, Athenian statesman and general [ca. 495–429]
Themistocles, Athenian statesman and general [524–459]
Thucydides, Greek historian [ca. 460–ca. 395]
Xenophon, Athenian soldier [ca. 430–354]
Xerxes I, king of Persia [520–465]
Xerxes II, king of Persia [ca. 5th c.]

SCIENCE

Hippocrates, Greek physician [ca. 460–ca. 370]
Ictinus, designed rebuilding of the Athenian Acropolis [mid-5th c.]
Callicrates, designed rebuilding of the Athenian Acropolis [mid-5th c.]
Protagoras, Greek mathematician and philosopher [ca. 490–420]

RELIGION/PHILOSOPHY

Anaxagoras, Greek philosopher from Asia Minor [ca. 500–428]
Democritus, Greek philosopher [ca. 460–ca. 370]
Empedocles, Greek philosopher [ca. 490–430]
Ezra, Hebrew scribe [ca. 5th c.]
Heraclitus, Greek philosopher [ca. 535–475]
Meh-Ti, Chinese philosopher [ca. 5th c.]
Mo-tzu, Chinese philosopher [ca. 470–391]
Parmenides, Greek philosopher [early 5th c.]
Plato, Greek philosopher [428–348]
Socrates, Greek philosopher [470–399]

LITERATURE

Bacchylides, Greek poet [ca. 507–ca. 450]
Pindar, Greek composer and poet [522–443]
Simonides of Ceos, Greek poet [ca. 556–468]

EURIPIDES

in an
hour

THE BIG THREE

Of the many tragedians practicing in Athens during the fifth century BCE, the work of only three of them has survived: Aeschylus, Sophocles, and Euripides. We know many others by name: Stone inscriptions recorded their victories in dramatic competitions, and their contemporaries wrote commentaries. But all their work has disappeared.

Why, then, should the work of only three remain? One answer might be that they represented the cream of the crop. Their plays were popular and received numerous productions after their first appearance in competition in Athens. They were produced in the outlying demes, or political units, of Athens and as far away as Sicily and the Athenian colonies that dotted the coast of Asia Minor. These productions would have needed copies of the original manuscripts, and those many copies, widely distributed, gave those plays a better chance of surviving than less popular plays. Additionally, schools used their plays as teaching tools for learning the art of rhetoric.

This is the core of the book. The essay places the playwright in the context of his world and analyzes the influences and inspirations within that world.

This leaves us with the Big Three of the Athenian fifth century. Of those three, we know a little about Aeschylus and Sophocles. We know next to nothing about Euripides.

BIOGRAPHICAL SOURCES

By the time people wanted to know the details of Euripides' life, it was too late: The documentation was gone. Letters to and from him, recollections of friends and family had been swept away by the tide of time, even as early as the age of Aristotle, midway in the fourth century. The majority of references to him that remain from the fifth century are from the Old Comedy tradition of Aristophanes and others.

These Old Comedy references were not meant to serve as biographical source material. It was part of the art of Old Comedy to be topical and to exaggerate. As David Kovacs, in the journal *Classical Philology*, noted: "For a joke to be worth making in Old Comedy, there need only be a slight resemblance between the actual person and his comic representation." Few public figures escaped lambasting by Old Comedy: politicians, military men, civic leaders, philosophers, poets, playwrights, even the gods. Everyone was a potential target, and the Classical Athenians must have loved it: It was part of their open society. Even Socrates likely laughed at his not-so-flattering representation onstage as "a quack scientist and a teacher of dishonest rhetoric" in Aristophanes' play *Clouds*.

Unfortunately, some have looked to Aristophanes' Old Comedy portrayals of Euripides for information about the playwright. For example, Euripides has been described as philosophically inclined, and his work has been characterized as anti-traditionalist. But, as David Kovacs has pointed out, these characterizations are likely based on those Old Comedy plays.

How closely did the comic representation resemble the real individual? In Aristophanes' *Frogs*, Aeschylus and Euripides are pitted against one another in Hades. The Aeschylus caricature is pompous, infatuated with the past, extremely old-fashioned, and a staunch moralist. Euripides is criticized for introducing slaves with speaking roles onto his stage and allowing the lowly and conventional on the stage as well.

The truth is that speaking slaves appear first in Aeschylus. Kovacs points out that in Aeschylus' *Oresteia*, Orestes' wet nurse describes her ward's toilet training — a liberty that Euripides would likely never take. Kovacs theorizes that since Euripides did make many innovations in the theater and is stylistically Aeschylus' opposite, whose approach was more traditional, Aristophanes chose to exaggerate those differences in his comedies. So he portrays Euripides as the atheist who values realism and the ordinary, whereas Aeschylus is pious and a champion of the heroic and of tragic decorum — all for comic effect but not necessarily representing the true beliefs and natures of the two men.

Equally suspect is the tendency of some critics to interpret the plays based on "facts" from unreliable biographical sources, or to see evidence of Euripides' own beliefs in his plays. Was he a woman hater? Only if Euripides' purpose in writing *Medea* was to demonstrate the evil of woman and Hippolytus' condemnation of woman in Euripides' play *Hippolytus* represents the playwright's own views. But there is no evidence on which to base such assumptions — no more (indeed far less) than we have for a similar misguided exercise in regard to Shakespeare.

WHAT WE DO KNOW

What, then, do we know about Euripides with reasonable certainty? Not much. He is said to have been born on the island of Salamis off the western coast of Greece on the very day of the Battle of Salamis, in which Athens finally defeated the Persian Empire under Xerxes. This is doubtful. Most likely this is an example of remembering a difficult date by shifting it to a date that is easily remembered. It is safe, however, to say that he was born in the 480s BCE. Precisely where is uncertain. As a boy he participated in a festival to Apollo Delios in Phyla, one of the demes of Athens. Another indisputable fact is that he won first prize in tragedy four times, one posthumously. We know, too, that he first entered the tragic competition at Athens in 455, and that his final entry was probably in 408. After that he left for Macedonia and the court of King Archelaus. It is said he left Athens a bitter man, possibly because he felt unappreciated. The more likely explanation is that life in Athens, after a war of more than two decades that Athens would soon lose, became too difficult. He died in 406. Two years later, Athens fell to Sparta in 404.

THE THEATER IN ATHENS

What did the theatrical space used by Aeschylus, Sophocles, Euripides, and their playwright colleagues look like in fifth century BCE? We know little about it or about the drama that was performed there — the Attic tragedies, Old Comedy plays, and satyr plays. The evidence has been swallowed up by the past. Scholars have been delving into the matter for centuries.

Of one thing, though, we are fairly certain. In the mid-sixth century, Athenian tragedy was performed in the *agora*, a marketplace or central gathering place for conducting business and socializing. From the agora in Athens, people could look east to the Acropolis. Our evidence is a drawing on a vase of the period. It appears that wooden bleachers were erected in the agora for the audience to sit on while watching a performance. Around the year 500 or so, performances were relocated to the Sacred Precinct of Dionysus on the south side of the Acropolis.

Although we have no proof, many have assumed that the spectators originally sat on the slope of the hill to the Acropolis to watch the performance. Perhaps wooden bleachers were erected for greater audience comfort, but even this is guesswork. It is roughly at this point that the general image of the Athenian Theater of Dionysus goes seriously awry. People assume that the theater suddenly blossomed into something resembling the theater at Epidaurus, but it wasn't until 350 BCE, 150 years later, that Epidaurus took shape.

THE *SKENE*

The theater at Epidaurus still exists today and is used for performing ancient Greek tragedies and comedies during summer festivals. The theater has a stone *skene*, a building across the back of the acting area that served as a room for changing costumes and also as a scenic backdrop for the play's action. It had one to three doors, and a *proskenion*, or row of pillars, stood in front of the doors. There may have been a second story to the *skene* and a *logion*, or roof, generally used for the appearance of gods at the end of a play. In front of the *skene* is the single most important part of the Greek theater, the *orchesis*, or orchestra, which literally means "dancing place." The orchestra was a round area of pounded earth circled with stones. Finally, there is the *theatron*, or "seeing place" — a vast stone auditorium built into the hillside. No archaeological evidence exists for the theater of Epidaurus in Athens until the 330s, when *stoa* (covered walkways), *skene*, and *theatron* were finally finished in stone.

We have evidence that the oldest stone *skene* in Athens appeared sometime between 421 and 415, thirty-four to forty years after Euripides first began writing plays. We also know that before those dates, the skene was constructed of wood. At the close of each festival, it was destroyed, and rebuilt the following year. We don't know when the wooden *skene* was first introduced, but there are clues. Aeschylus' *Oresteia*, first performed in 458, was the first play that required a *skene*. Conceivably, the *skene* could have existed earlier in the century for a play that no longer exists. In any event, we know that Euripides' first existing play, *Alcestis*, in 438, calls for a *skene*. So do his remaining nineteen existing plays.

THE ACTING AREA IN ATHENS

Was there a raised acting area in front of the *skene* for *Oresteia?* It's possible, but only in the late fifth and early fourth centuries do depictions of a low, raised platform appear on vase paintings. This platform, raised about a meter (roughly forty inches) with a flight of steps in the center, suggests that the action was not confined to the platform but spilled out into the orchestra circle. This still tells us nothing about the positioning of theatrical action in the earlier period from the late sixth to well into the fifth century. Nothing short of archaeological evidence could do that, and of that there is none.

But would such a raised level have been useful? Spectators looked down on the action of the play from a steeply raked *theatron*. Even the first row of seats, the thrones for priests and dignitaries, was above the ground-level playing area.

THE ATHENIAN ORCHESTRA

We also have no evidence regarding the original shape of the early Athenian orchestra, where the chorus sang and danced. Some smaller outlying Attic theaters late in the fifth century had orchestras that were not circular. Both Thorikos and Trachones had tiny provincial deme theaters in which the audience sat on wooden benches arranged in a rectangle or trapezoid close to the acting area. Possibly the early theater at Athens had a similar rectangular or trapezoidal shape, though on a much grander scale.

Some scholars maintain that there is no evidence for a circular orchestra in Athens before the 330s. Others argue that the choreography performed by the chorus required a circular area, so there must have been one from the start. In any event, we will never know what the original Athenian orchestra looked like because all the archaeological evidence has been destroyed.

SEATING CAPACITY IN ATHENS

The size of the Greek theater varied widely. One thing is certain: The early Theater of Dionysus in Athens, though not the largest Greek theater, must have been massive. It had to accommodate the male citizenry who attended the performances, in addition to visitors from outlying demes, not to mention important foreign visitors. The capacity of the theater has been judged to be somewhere between 15,000 and 20,000. Size, however, meant that spectators were seated a distance away from the theatrical event, which the surviving stone *theatron* at Athens demonstrates. It rises to touch the fortified walls of the Acropolis many hundreds of feet away.

THE MASK AND MULTIPLE CASTING

It's possible that masks were used in the Classical Greek theater because of the great distance between spectators and actors. Some have even speculated that masks also served as megaphones to amplify the actors' voices. A more obvious reason is that masks had long been a part of Greek culture and were used widely in cult ceremonies. Adolescent rites of passage from Sparta used rather grotesque masks, and the cult of Demeter and Despoina at Lycosura is known for using animal masks. The mask in Greek tragedy most likely derives its use from the cult rituals of Dionysus, the god of the theater.

Masks, which were generally made of linen and covered the entire head, did, however, give the actors a greater presence onstage. The masks represented types rather than individuals, and they were useful for disguising a male actor in a female role. (Women were excluded from theatrical performances.) But perhaps the most compelling reason for the mask was financial. The mask enabled one actor to play multiple parts, which meant only two to three actors needed to be hired for all the speaking roles. Double and even triple casting was used often and, one must assume, to good effect.

Even though the primary reason for only three actors was very likely economic, to have the same actor play, for example, the roles of Clytemnestra, Electra, and Athena in *Oresteia* offered artistic and dramatic resonances that are far-reaching and intriguing. As for the numbers of nonspeaking actors onstage, there was no limit, and exciting stage effects with scores of "extras" would not have been unusual.

THE CHORUS

The importance of the chorus cannot be overestimated. In Athens especially, there was a long tradition (even before tragedy) of choruses performing the dithyramb, an ancient Greek hymn sung and danced in honor of Dionysus, in competitions. Even in the days of tragedy, separate competitions were devoted to the dithyramb in which all ten demes of Athens participated. In Aeschylus' day, the tragic chorus numbered twelve. Then Sophocles added three more for a total of fifteen.

In his *Tragedy in Athens*, David Wiles argues convincingly that the choreographed movement of the chorus was not in straight lines or highly formalized and that the chorus was very active. For example, when chorus members representing the Young Theban Women in Aeschylus' *Seven Against Thebes* first enter, they express their terror of the war just outside their city gates with agitated, disorderly movements. In Sophocles' *Oedipus at Colonus*, there is a similar entry by the chorus of Old Men, who dart wildly about the orchestra in search of the intruder into the Sacred Grove.

Wiles further proposes that the chorus acted out the subject of each choral ode in a choreographed dance and also the subjects of others' narration. For example, during the Persian Herald's speech in *Persians*, the chorus mimed his description of the defeat of the Persian forces in the naval battle at Salamis. Other examples from Euripides' plays are the narrative in *Bacchae* describing the death of Pentheus, the destruction of Hippolytus' chariot by the bull from the sea in *Hippolytus*, and the sacrifice of Iphigenia at Aulis in *Iphigenia*.

Wiles' brilliant insights indicate the broad and important role the choruses performed in Athenian tragedies. This expanded role explains why Athenians who attended the theater spoke of going to the choreography rather than to the play.

MUSIC AND TRAGEDY

We know very little about the music of Archaic and Classical Greece. Some music scores survive, but they are largely fragmentary and date from the Hellenistic period or later. The Greeks were knowledgeable about a great many musical instruments, especially from their eastern neighbors, but they adopted only two types: a stringed instrument (lyre) and a wind instrument or pipe (aulos). The aulos was not a flute but a reed instrument, using either a single or double reed. In fifth-century tragedy, the double-pipe aulos was the instrument of choice to accompany the musical sections of the dramatic action. Drums may also have been used; for example in *Bacchae*, drums are frequently mentioned.

Music in fifth-century tragedy was of primary importance. Every one of the extant tragedies has a number of choral sections (usually five) built into it. The sections, during which the singing and dancing chorus holds the center of attention in the orchestra, are generally short. In addition, there are sections in which two characters sing their lines or spoken dialogue alternates with recitative or song. The latter are often between a character or characters and the chorus. These sections exist in the same time frame as the scenes of exclusively spoken dialogue. P. E. Easterling suggests, in the journal *Yale Classical Studies*, that the sung sections were likely meant "to intensify emotion or to give a scene a ritual dimension, as in a shared lament or song of celebration." How much music was used in performance is not known, but it is intriguing to speculate that its role was enormous and went far beyond those sections of the plays that call specifically for music.

THEATER FESTIVALS OF ATHENS

What we know about the production of tragedy in Greece is almost totally confined to Attica, though other areas were also active producers. From the close of the sixth and throughout the fifth century, tragedy was primarily performed as part of the Great, or City, Dionysia in Athens, a yearly festival in honor of Dionysus that happened every March. Tragedy was also a part of the Rural Dionysia during the winter months when bad weather made access to Athens difficult. But tragedy was not the sole reason for these festivals. They also scheduled processions, sacrifices in the theater, libations, the parade of war orphans, and the performance of dithyramb poetry and comedy. The final day was devoted to reviewing the festival and awarding prizes.

Three tragedians competed with three plays each plus a satyr play, all chosen by the *archon*, a state official who also appointed the three *choregoi*. These three men were responsible for financing and training the choruses. The actors and playwrights were paid by the state. One judge from each of the ten tribes, or demes, of Athens was chosen to decide the winners of the competition, and the winning playwright was crowned with a wreath of ivy in the theater. Until about the middle of the fifth century, each tragedy was comprised of three plays on a similar theme, followed by a satyr or comic play. Eventually each of the three plays, as well as the satyr, had a different subject and was independent of the others.

And then there was Dionysus — god of theater.

DIONYSUS: GOD OF THEATER

What had the theater to do with Dionysus, and Dionysus with the theater? How did the two become one and mutually express one? Why is Dionysus an appropriate representative of the art of drama, and in particular of tragedy?

Some scholars believe that Dionysus was the original subject of the dithyramb chorus. Tragedy developed out of the dithyramb, and as Aristotle conjectured, tragedy simply took Dionysus along. We are less certain now, however, about this explanation. Athenian tragedy dealt with a broad range of subjects, not just Dionysus: Though Dionysus plays a significant part in tragedy, he has a lot of competition.

Perhaps it is Dionysus' otherness that makes him an appropriate representative for tragedy. He can transform into animate and inanimate objects and cannot be pinned down. His cult ritual, which existed long before tragedy, has aspects similar to drama: masks for disguise and ecstatic possession — the ability to assume alternate personalities. He is associated with song and with dance in partnership with satyrs and maenads. These are only a few of the possibilities that may have led to this god's association with drama.

The satyr play provides one clear link with Dionysus. From the late sixth and well into the fifth century, the satyr play was an important part of tragedy, and satyrs — those lusty half-goat, half-man creatures — were closely associated with Dionysus. Easterling notes that dithyramb poetry, the satyr play, and tragedy all share song and dance and that the satyr play " was the most obviously Dionysiac element, since the chorus of satyrs, far more than any other choral group, was explicitly and by definition part of the god's entourage, and satyrs of various types, as we have known from vase-paintings, had been associated with Dionysus well before the dramatic festivals were established."

DIONYSUS AND THE MASK

The mask, used in both Greek tragedies and in Dionysian cult rituals, provides a key link between Dionysus and the theater. Dionysus is a god of escape, and the mask is one means for escaping reality. But who would think of Greek tragedy as escapism, a way to leave reality behind? And yet despite the grim subject matter of Greek tragedy, it is still entertainment, removed from real life and providing escape. Greek tragedy is filled with devices that separate it from daily life, an important one being the language of the plays. The Athenians didn't use the diction and vocabulary of Attic tragedy in their daily speech, just as the Elizabethan playgoer didn't use the language of Shakespeare's stage on the street. This use of more formal, poetic language in plays is especially true in Aeschylus and Sophocles, perhaps less so in Euripides. In addition to language, music, the elaborate choreography of the chorus, and masks all provided distance between reality and the play.

The mask also permitted an actor to take on not just one but as many roles as needed in the course of the tetralogy or trilogy: the three tragic plays and the final comic satyr play. In the early days of tragedy, there was only one actor hired for all the speaking parts. Then Aeschylus added a second actor. Sophocles wrote for three actors. But no matter how many actors were hired for the play, each was required to play as many speaking roles as the play called for. One actor could play four or even five roles, including female parts.

Pentheus, for example, in Euripides' play *Bacchae*, also plays his mother, Agave, who at the end enters carrying her son's severed head. No Athenian in that Theater of Dionysus could have failed to be aware of the game openly being played on him, and he must have relished it. He knew by the timbre of a voice or by delivery that Pentheus was now (in the terrible/wonderful deception that was theater) his mother carrying his own head. The illusion of reality was deliberately broken, which said to the audience that this is not life as you know it. Finally, at the end was the down-and-dirty ribaldry of the satyr play, which sent audience members home laughing — just in case they fell into the trap of taking things a bit too seriously.

There is one further link between Dionysus and the mask. As we know from paintings on Greek pottery that depict Dionysian rituals (in particular the large craters for storing wine), Dionysus was frequently "present" at cult rituals in the form of a large suspended or supported mask. This mask, representing Dionysus, suggests that he was there to observe the playing out of his many aspects during the ritual.

Similarly, at the beginning of every City Dionysia at Athens, a large statue of Dionysus was placed dead center in the *theatron*. There, he oversaw the day's theatrical representations of himself in the form of dance, ecstatic possession, and disguise through masks. He watches himself onstage in every act, from the tragic to the playful. Like the gods in various of his plays, he is manipulating the action and the fate of his characters — like Aphrodite and Artemis in *Hippolytus*, Athena in *Ajax*, and Dionysus himself in *Bacchae*.

Then, in the final satyr play, he watched debauchery, drunkenness, and general ribaldry.

DIONYSUS, SEX, AND DEATH

The sexual aspect of Dionysus and his cult is undeniable. His most formidable symbol is the giant phallus. This ritual instrument, a sign of generation and fertility, was prominently displayed and carried through the streets in processions on various holidays. At women's festivals, a smaller version was placed in a cradle and treated like a baby.

Sex was a common subject in Attic tragedies. It appears as both a motif and a catalyst. Attic tragedy could scarcely function without it: Think of Phaedra and Hippolytus, the Suppliants and their Egyptian suitors, Medea and Jason, Heracles and Deianira, or Pentheus and Dionysus. In each of these relationships, sex is dark, disruptive, and tragic. It leads inevitably to the final resolution of all problems — death. Count no man happy till he is dead.

Dionysus and death? How can the Dionysus who gives wine, who causes milk to flow from the earth and honey to spout from his ritual *thyrsus* (a staff of giant fennel covered with ivy and topped with a pine cone), who dances happily with his satyrs and maenads have anything to do with death? Dionysus is linked with liberation and escape, and death is, after all, the only total escape. It is the only true liberation from pain, dishonor, and fear and the only pure pleasure — a kind of rapture in destruction. At the same time, it is the paradoxical absence of pleasure in nonbeing. Death is a frequent occurrence in Athenian tragedy — and particularly in Euripides. It is often the only answer to the dark shadow of sex.

DIONYSUS AND TRAGEDY

Dionysus is the god of the theater because he is everything: light/dark, hot/cold, wet/dry, sound/silence, pleasure/pain, life/death. He lures his Athenian audience into his theater to escape from reality by raising life — through language, music, dance, and masks — to a level that transcends reality. And he does so with a smile. He is, after all, known as the "smiling god" — though his smile is often demonic. He knows what his audience doesn't know: The play is not an escape from but an amplification of reality. Because the play mirrors him, it mirrors all things, encompassing both life — fertility and sex — and death. Dionysus' link with these Attic tragedies is inevitable and clear: In the plays, sex, life's greatest pleasure, is often the catalyst that leads to death — the only answer and possible resolution to the play's dilemma and the greatest pleasure of all.

ALCESTIS

Although *Alcestis* was the nineteenth play written by Euripides, it is the earliest of his ninety or so plays to survive. It was produced at the City Dionysia in Athens in 438, when Euripides was in his middle to late forties. It was the fourth, and final, play in a tragic tetralogy, a position that was traditionally occupied by a satyr play. And here is where the problems regarding *Alcestis* begin.

The satyr play was a light comedy. In it a chorus of satyrs and a cast of tragic heroes performed a send-up of a serious mythic event. In the old days — even as late as mid-fifth-century Athens — a tragic trilogy united by a single mythic theme preceded the satyr play. An example is Aeschylus' *Oresteia* from 458. Although the satyr play that concluded the *Oresteia* is lost, its subject was the House of Atreus.

At some point, the three tragic plays ceased to be connected thematically and evolved into three independent tragedies, followed by an independent satyr play. The three tragedies that preceded *Alcestis* (*The Cretan Women, Alcmaeon in Psophis,* and *Telephus*) were not united; all four plays had different subjects. Furthermore, *Alcestis* is a dramatic play — and not a traditional, comic satyr play.

This fact has disturbed critics and commentators since antiquity. Why is a basically tragic drama filling the space occupied by a satyr play? What's more, *Alcestis* has elements that simply don't belong in an Athenian tragedy; for one, it has a happy ending. This didn't much bother the audience in the Theater of Dionysus in Athens on that March afternoon in 438. It was awarded second prize in competition with Euripides' elder contemporary, Sophocles, who came in first. Scholars, however, continue to explore the *Alcestis* conundrum.

Tragedy and Tragic Endings

Must tragedies always have a tragic ending? Aristotle, of course, would say yes. In his *Poetics*, he declares that tragic action must progress from good fortune to bad. *Alcestis*, however, does precisely the opposite: It begins tragically and ends happily. Euripides, however, wasn't able to benefit from Aristotle's advice or read his *Poetics*, as Aristotle wouldn't be born for another fifty-four years.

So what did Euripides have in mind? Among his nineteen existing plays, and the seven each of Aeschylus and Sophocles, none is like *Alcestis*, although Euripides does have several other plays with happy endings — *Andromache, Ion, Helen,* and *Iphigenia in Tauris*. Euripides in general took liberties with the tragic form. Most Classical Greek playwrights drew their subject matter from myths, epics, and sagas from a few royal houses. Euripides, however, frequently chose obscure plots for his tragedies, perhaps because he felt the genre had become too predictable and he wanted to use the traditional structure of tragedy in new ways.

The happy ending isn't the only unusual feature of *Alcestis*. As critics have frequently commented, the play goes beyond the mythic. It is full of folklore and fairy-tale situations that are absent in other tragedies of the fifth century. Perhaps other playwrights considered fairy tales inappropriate subject matter for tragedy. In *Alcestis*, Euripides has combined myth and folktale.

Alcestis is based on mythic events that happened before the start of the play. Years earlier, Apollo had been exiled from Olympus for nine years and spent a year of that time in service to King Admetus. Admetus treated him well, and as a reward, Apollo granted Admetus the privilege of living a longer than average life. To achieve this, Admetus must, however, find someone to take his place when Death comes to claim him. At the start of the play, the time of Ademtus' death has arrived, and his devoted wife Alcestis steps forward to die in his place.

The myth of Apollo and his servitude to Admetus was known as far back as the eighth century in the work of Hesiod. But there is no sign anywhere before Euripides' tragedy of Alcestis' self-sacrifice. D. J. Conacher, in *Euripidean Drama: Myth, Theme and Structure*, suggests that Alcestis wasn't always attached to the Apollo-Admetus story. The story of her sacrifice and rescue from the underworld began, he believes, as a folktale.

The play is full of other events that are more fairy tale than myth: Heracles wrestling with Death at the grave of Alcestis and later stealing her from Death, and the battle between the forces of light and good (Apollo and Heracles) against the forces of evil (the Fates and Death) with the good triumphing.

MEDEA

Medea was first produced in 431 and won third prize in the competition at the City Dionysia in Athens. It was a good spring that year; things appeared to be going well. Athens was at the peak of her power, and her empire was a mighty force to be reckoned with both on land and at sea. Colonies flourished. The arts, architecture, sculpture, philosophy, and science were triumphant. Tragedy was in its glory days. Democracy, that sixth-century invention, was at its height. All these triumphs had been set in motion sixty years earlier when Athens, which had been at the mercy of the Persians since 514, finally defeated the invaders in 490 at Marathon. Then the final Persian defeat came in 480 with the stupendous naval victory at Salamis off the western coast of Athens.

Athens was a proud city, and Euripides paid it homage in one of the choral odes in his *Medea.* The tragedy is that when he wrote his hymn to Athenian greatness, little did Euripides know that it was the last moment when such praise could be lavished. Athens had reached a pinnacle of her power and glory, the greatest the world had ever known. But it was the beginning of the end. Later that year, the clouds of war would roll over the landscape and the devastation of the Peloponnesian War would begin. Athens' decline was slow at first, but eventually became precipitous, and in 404 the city fell to Sparta.

Chronicler of His Time

Aristophanes' comedy *Frogs* was first produced in 405, one year before Athens' fall. In it, the author has a conservative Aeschylus rake Euripides over the coals for his lack of patriotism. In response to the charge of demoralizing the Athenian public in his tragedies during the devastating war (for Euripides saw what was happening early on), he counters (in Jeffrey Henderson's translation) with:

> I taught these people how to talk . . . and how to apply
> subtle rules and square off their words, to think, to see, to

understand, to be quick on their feet, to scheme, to see the bad in others, to think of all aspects of everything . . . by staging everyday scenes, things we're used to, things that we live with, things that I wouldn't have got away with falsifying, because these spectators knew them as well as I and could have exposed my faulty art. . . . That's how I encouraged these people to think, by putting rationality and critical thinking into my art, so that now they grasp and really understand everything, especially how to run their households better than they used to, and how to keep an eye on things.

Euripides saw his city and its people falling apart, and he portrayed what he saw in his plays. But that reporting made him unpopular with his countrymen.

The feel of war was in the air even when *Medea* was first played. But this time the war would not be the near-mythic heroic struggle for survival that was the Persian War. Athenians would soon learn that war was not glorious or idealistic. It was not the sport of heroes or the training ground for manhood. It was a petty, vulgar struggle for national domination. Euripides' audience wanted to see heroes on their stage, but Euripides gave them none. The Jasons, the Neoptolemuses of the past were now as petty as the people who watched them. These are just a few of the bubbles that Euripides burst, and his audience didn't welcome the news.

Athens on the Verge of Collapse

No one can say that Euripides' *Medea* predicts a world on the verge of collapse. It was a bit too early for that in 431, even though the Peloponnesian War would begin within months. Rather, the play deals with specific domestic issues, not issues of state, which strongly suggests that *Medea* is a commentary on the relations between the sexes. That relationship reveals a major flaw in Athenian society.

Athenian men were completely dominant and central to the society. Half of Athens' citizens, its women, were in something like domestic chains. That exaggerated insistence on male prerogative in every area of Athenian life was the undisputed reason for the collapse in 404 of Athens' social, moral, and political structure.

Society was deteriorating. In his third volume of *History of the Peloponnesian War*, Thucydides speaks of this general deterioration of character in the Greek world at large in 427: "The simple way of looking at things, which is so much the mark of a noble nature, was regarded as a ridiculous quality and soon ceased to exist."

Though the family, not the state, is the subject of *Medea*, it, much like Shakespeare's *Hamlet*, reflects not only the dissolution of a family but the end of an era and is full of images of decay. In that sense, *Medea* foretells Athens' decline, not only physically but morally.

HIPPOLYTUS

Hippolytus was performed at the City Dionysia at Athens in 428. It won first prize, a distinction Euripides achieved only four times in his long and productive life. As it happens, the *Hippolytus* that won in that fourth year of the Peloponnesian War was Euripides' second attempt at the tale — and is the play we have now. Sometime earlier he had written a version of the same material with the same title, but it failed to please its spectators and caused something of a scandal because of its portrayal of Phaedra. The conventional Athenian audience was shocked by his portrayal of Phaedra as a passionate and aggressive female who shamelessly propositions her stepson, Hippolytus. In this male-dominated society, respectable Athenian women were expected to conduct themselves with strict decorum and modesty.

In the story, Hippolytus, the illegitimate son of Theseus, King of Athens, has sworn chastity and his allegiance to Artemis, the chaste goddess of the hunt. He refuses to revere Aphrodite, goddess of sexual love. The angry goddess takes revenge by making Phaedra, his stepmother, fall madly in love with him. Phaedra confesses her feelings for her stepson to her nurse. The nurse in turn tells Hippolytus, but makes him swear an oath that he will tell no one. When Phaedra finds out that her secret is out, she hangs herself rather than face dishonor and leaves a note behind indicating that Hippolytus is the cause of her suicide. Theseus returns, finds the dead body of his wife, reads her note, and assumes that Hippolytus has raped her. He angrily accuses Hippolytus, who is unable to defend himself and tell the truth because of the oath he swore. In anger, Theseus exiles and curses his son and calls upon Poseidon to enforce the curse. Hippolytus departs in his chariot, when a bull — Poseidon — roars out of the sea and frightens his horses. He wrecks his chariot and lies dying. At the end, Theseus finally learns the truth from Artemis, and Hippolytus absolves his father of blame for his death and dies.

The Flight Toward Purity

The central issue of *Hippolytus* is generally considered to be sex, and of course, it is. But more narrowly defined, it is about avoiding sex, the flight *from* sexual encounter. That flight from sex is, in the case of both Hippolytus and Phaedra, the flight toward purity.

Hippolytus' life — for all its apparent calm and peace of mind, for all his devotion to Artemis as goddess of chastity — is a snakepit of terror. He deeply fears sex, fears its power over him. For Hippolytus, purity is a façade to hide his sexual fears and anger. The degree to which he insists on his abstinence and his devotion to Artemis betrays how fragile and weak he is. He seeks honor, but only on his own terms. He seeks reputation, but it is a narrow definition of reputation he sets for himself.

Phaedra, too, seeks to maintain honor and reputation in her flight from sex. She is as terrified of her overpowering sexual desire for Hippolytus as Hippolytus is of sex in general. In Phaedra, honor and reputation are foremost — not only hers, but her children's and husband's as well. It isn't sex, as such, that she fears; it is the illicit sex with her stepson that will vilify her. For Phaedra, purity is a moral principle, versus Hippolytus, for whom purity is escape.

Phaedra, a married woman with a family, has accepted sex as a vital part of being and lives a balanced life. She is a woman for whom honor and reputation are the natural signs of a life well lived. She *chooses* them freely; she loves honor, she loves reputation, and she is nothing if not honorable and respectable. But Aphrodite, the goddess of sexual love, has forced her into a demeaning sexual situation. Phaedra's desire for Hippolytus is not of her choosing. She is divinely possessed — a pawn in Aphrodite's plot to hound Hippolytus to death for his failure to honor her by rejecting his sexual side. Phaedra's every action is to fight that possession.

Hippolytus, on the other hand, is not divinely possessed. He is possessed by his overwhelming fear of sex, a fear that prompts his every action. Even though he insists on honor and reputation and purity, he has chosen them out of fear, not freely (which does not imply, however, that honor and reputation are not as natural to his nature as they are to Phaedra's). He, in fact, says as much about himself in his speech to Artemis' image in the first scene.

Cloistered Virtue

What makes Hippolytus a "pure" individual? What makes him insist on his armor of virtue? There are several possibilities.

First, we must consider the position of women in fifth-century Athens, at the time Euripides wrote *Hippolytus*. Women, to put it bluntly, were equated with slaves: "Women and slaves" was the going phrase at the time. Women had little freedom outside their own houses. Both before and after marriage, they were denied general public and social freedom. They were, furthermore, considered inferior to males. A century later, Aristotle still upheld this viewpoint, and it has been with us ever since. Women were thought to be devious and untrustworthy.

Hippolytus is an extreme product of this anti-woman culture. He needs to be the stereotypic superior male, and he maintains his superiority and purity by avoiding relations with women. Though bisexuality was all but taken for granted for the young male in classical Athens, it's likely that Hippolytus is not even, at least in practice, homosexual. He protects himself from sex entirely. He retreats from life. He constructs his own reality with the band of young male friends we see in the play's first scene (his compatriots in purity). Poet John Milton's phrase "cloistered virtue" accurately describes Hippolytus' brand of purity, which he maintains by avoiding the expectations and temptations that everyone else faces daily. What is the worth of a virtue that avoids temptation by locking itself away?

Family Relations

There are also private, familial concerns that bear on Hippolytus. First of all, Hippolytus is a bastard, a fact that is mentioned frequently in the play by almost everyone, including Hippolytus himself. This condition has wounded him deeply. He is not heir apparent to his father Theseus' throne; Phaedra's children will be the inheritors. Hippolytus has nothing to look forward to. He is an outcast, the odd man out, and by retreating from the world, he further ostracizes himself.

Theseus is his father in name only; he is forever off on a new adventure and is absent for most of the play. Furthermore, Theseus is profoundly intimidating to his son. He is a hero of the first magnitude, on par with that greatest of all Greek heroes, Heracles. And like Heracles, his heroic adventures are in service to civilization. His frequent appearance in Greek tragedy alone confirms his position in Athens. Theseus was also a notorious womanizer, the Don Juan of the

Greek world, and Hippolytus is the result of one of Theseus' many affairs. His mother was Queen of the Amazons.

As hero and seducer, Theseus is a major threat to his son's development. How does a son live up to a father who is a near-mythic hero and a sexual athlete? Hippolytus doesn't have an easy time of it. He is also intimidated by the social reality around him, with all its attendant conflicts. Why should he be a sexual being when that leads to commitments and the inevitable male-female social tensions and conflicts he sees everywhere around him?

Hippolytus leaves society and constructs his own world. Behind his façade of purity, he hides his terror of what most revolts him — sex. Given provocation, he is ready to erupt into violence at any time, as indeed he does in his violent misogynistic speech aimed at Phaedra. Hatred of women is what motivates him. That hatred is every bit as powerful as that of Aphrodite's hatred of him for his rejection of her. He is, in short, a considerably less controlled version of the conventional phallocentric Athenian male.

ANDROMACHE

Athenian tragedians found most of their subject matter in the poems of the so-called Epic Cycle of earlier Greek antiquity. Most of these poems and much of the early lyric poetry has been lost, however, and we can only guess what form of this material reached the fifth-century tragedians. However, all the characters in Euripides' *Andromache*, with the exception of Hermione, come from this epic tradition.

Neoptolemus, the chief figure in the myth on which Euripides based his play, is mentioned frequently by Homer. In the *Iliad*, he is spoken of only once, as the son of Achilles, but in the *Odyssey*, he is given greater attention. There he is said to have returned from Troy to be a prospective husband of Hermione. On a visit to Hades, Odysseus tells the shade of Achilles about his son's accomplishments at Troy. Later epic tradition informs us of his prowess in the final stage of the war at Troy. He participated in the capture of the citadel. He brutally murdered the aged Priam at the altar to which he had fled for safety. He is also credited with throwing Astyanax, the infant son of Hector and Andromache, to his death from the walls of Troy.

Of his death there are various versions, though he always dies at Delphi. Pindar, in his *Paean 6*, from about 490, has him die at the instigation of Apollo for having killed the aged Priam at the altar of Zeus. In *Nemian 7*, however, Pindar adopts, or invents, another version that has him killed at Delphi in an argument over the flesh of sacrificial victims. There were many other versions, including that of Euripides, which may be original with him.

In the *Iliad* Homer refers to Andromache as the noble and loving wife of Hector. Homer is particularly moving when he describes Andromache and her husband contemplating their probable fate. Hector speaks to his wife about her life as a slave when Troy falls:

> You will live in Argos, weaving at the loom at another woman's command, and carrying water from a foreign spring, from Messeïs or Hypereia, much against your will, but compulsion will lie harsh upon you. And someone seeing you with your tears falling will say: "This is the wife of Hektor, who was always the best warrior of the horse-taming Trojans, when they were fighting over Ilios." That is what they will say: and for you there will be renewed misery, that you have lost such a husband to protect you from the day of slavery.

Hermione is mentioned by Homer and Hesiod. Homer says she was the only child of Menelaus and Helen. Hesiod says they had two. Homer also mentions that her wedding to Neoptolemus was arranged by Menelaus. Homer, Hesiod, and possibly Sappho, in a fragment, speak of her as having inherited some of her mother's beauty.

The three remaining characters, Peleus, Menelaus, and Orestes, are legendary figures of considerable distinction in the epic tradition.

However, in *Andromache*, Menelaus and Orestes are given a dressing-down: Menelaus is reviled because he is a Spartan. Orestes is likely demoted because he was in league with Menelaus. This treatment wasn't unusual in fifth-century Athenian tragedy and is a reasonable reaction, given the political realities of the time. When the play was first produced, around 425, Athens and Sparta were battling each other in the Peloponnesian War.

The Tale

Andromache takes place several years after the Trojan War. The scene is the palace of Neoptolemus, son of Achilles, at Thetideion in Thessaly. The palace is not far from Phthia, where Neoptolemus' grandfather Peleus is king. Following the Greek victory at Troy, Neoptolemus was awarded Andromache, widow of the valiant Trojan warrior Hector, as his war prize. She became his mistress, by whom he had a son named Molossos. However, in his need to produce legitimate male heirs, he married Hermione, the daughter of Menelaus and Helen of Sparta.

Hermione is jealous of Andromache, who is now her slave. While her husband is away at Delphi, Hermione plans to murder Andromache and Molossos. She summons her father, Menelaus, from Sparta to serve as her accomplice.

At the opening of the play, Andromache has spirited her son away into safekeeping and is a suppliant at the altar dedicated to Thetis. Menelaus, meanwhile, has found the boy. He threatens to slaughter Molossos unless Andromache surrenders herself. When she does surrender, he tells her that Hermione, not him, will decide the boy's fate. Just as Andromache and Molossos are about to be slain, the aged King Peleus, grandfather of Neoptolemus, arrives. He condemns Menelaus for his action and his Spartan cruelty, and then scornfully dismisses him. Menelaus exits. Peleus unbinds Andromache and the boy and takes them back with him to nearby Phthia. After Menelaus exits, a hysterical Hermione enters, terrified that Neoptolemus will kill her on his return for her attempted murder of Andromache and her son.

As if in answer to her prayers, her cousin Orestes enters. He is presumably on his way to Zeus' oracle at Dodona, and while in Thessaly he has decided to look up his relative. She tells him of her failed plans. He reveals to her that he already knew of the trouble she was in. He has come to take her off to safety and to marry her. As it happens, she was originally promised to Orestes by her father, Menelaus, before the war. That arrangement was altered when Menelaus gave her instead to Neoptolemus as a war prize for bringing down Troy. Orestes then announces that he has already organized a plot to kill Neoptolemus at Delphi, where he has gone to seek forgiveness for an earlier affront to Apollo.

With Orestes and Hermione gone, Peleus returns (possibly with Andromache and Molossos in tow). He has heard rumors that Hermione has fled. The chorus confirms that reality and warns that his grandson Neoptolemus is in danger for his life at Delphi. Before Peleus can send a slave to Delphi to warn Neoptolemus, a messenger arrives with news of his death. Orestes had spread the rumor that Neoptolemus had come to plunder Delphi; the angered Delphians then killed him in the precinct of Apollo's temple. No sooner is the report concluded than the body of Neoptolemus is carried in. Peleus is deeply upset by the news and laments that his house is nearly destroyed.

Euripides then uses one of his favored devices — the deus ex machina. The sea goddess Thetis appears out of nowhere to resolve the action as well as to bring needed solace to Peleus, Thetis' former husband. As for his house, it is not destroyed; Molossos is, after all, Neoptolemus' son. Andromache, who is now free, will marry Priam's son Helenus, Hector's brother, and live in Molossia. Molossos will be the region's first king as well as the father to a distinguished line of kings. As for Peleus, he will become an immortal and live with Thetis in perpetuity in the kingdom of the sea god Poseidon, her father.

A Matter of Revenge

Andromache was written and performed sometime between 427 and 425. It reflects the attitude not only of Athens but of Greek society in general during the first years of the almost three-decade-long Peloponnesian War between Sparta and Athens. Thucydides wrote in his *History of the Peloponnesian War* that revenge became a national epidemic. Revenge is surely the most pervasive element in the play. Every action is motivated by revenge: Hermione on Andromache, Menelaus on Neoptolemus, Orestes on Neoptolemus. Of revenge in those years, Thucydides wrote, years later:

> Revenge was more important than self-preservation. And if pacts of mutual security were made, they were entered into by the two parties only in order to meet some temporary difficulty, and remained in force only so long as there was no other weapon available. When the chance came, the one who first seized it boldly, catching his enemy off his guard, enjoyed a revenge that was all the sweeter for having been taken, not openly, but because of a breach of faith. It was safer that way, it was considered, and at the same time a victory won by treachery gave one a title for superior intelligence. And indeed most people are more ready to call villainy cleverness than simple-mindedness honesty. They are proud of the first quality and ashamed of the second.

What else can we think of in this regard? Menelaus gained advantage in dissolving Sparta's alliance with Neoptolemus and Phthia. Neoptolemus, and therefore Phthia, is out of favor with Delphi. That is not good for Menelaus and Sparta. Furthermore, his marriage to Hermione has produced no legitimate heirs. So what else is there for Sparta to do but break that alliance (even if it means the death of Neoptolemus) in favor of an alliance between the new Argos about to be founded by Orestes, Menelaus' nephew? That alliance would be sealed, as such matters frequently were, with a marriage.

The cruelty of Menelaus and Orestes, as well as Hermione in her plan to murder Andromache and Molossos, can be clearly seen. Thucydides saw it. He reported the changes taking place in Greece as a result of the Corcyrean revolution of 427, just before the writing of *Andromache*. He saw a precipitous decline in standards of morality and behavior. Bear in mind that Euripides was not reflecting Thucydides, who hadn't written his history at the time of the play. Euripides was reporting in his play what he observed going on around him as the war raged. As Thucydides wrote:

> To fit in with the change of events, words, too, had to change their usual meanings. What used to be described as a thoughtless act of aggression was now regarded as the courage one would expect to find in a party member; to think of the future and wait was merely another way of saying one was a coward; any idea of moderation was just an attempt to disguise one's unmanly character; ability to understand a question from all sides meant that one was totally unfitted for action. Fanatical enthusiasm was the mark of a real man, and to plot against an enemy behind his back was perfectly legitimate self-defense. Anyone who held violent opinions could always be trusted, and anyone who objected to them became a suspect. To plot successfully was a sign of intelligence, but it was still cleverer to see that a plot was hatching. If one attempted to provide against having to do either, one was disrupting the unity of the party and acting out of fear of the opposition. In short, it was equally praiseworthy to get one's blow in first against someone who was going to do wrong, and to denounce someone who had no intention of doing any wrong at all.

Andromache is a play that so thoroughly mirrors the temper and obsessions of its time that even its apparent fragmentation might well be Euripides' way of suggesting the fragmentation of the world he lived in.

HECUBA

As is true of most of the existing plays of Euripides, we have only an approximate date for *Hecuba*. It was written and produced somewhere around 425–24, which puts it, like *Andromache*, within the first decade of the Peloponnesian War.

Hecuba, although less well known today, was popular in its day, which is not surprising as it covers emotions that its contemporary audience would have been familiar with: the pain that accompanies the destruction of cities — dislocation, homelessness, the annihilation of the male population, and the enslavement of women and children. Hecuba, Queen of Troy and the wife of King Priam, embodies all the horrors and suffering of war: She is a captive of the Greeks. Her husband is dead, her city destroyed. Her son Hector was brutally killed by Achilles, and Polymestor has betrayed and murdered her son Polydorus. As the play opens, she has just learned that her daughter Polyxena will be sacrificed at the tomb of Achilles, her son's killer, and her daughter Cassandra, a virgin-priestess to Apollo, is to become Agamemnon's concubine. She herself is destined to be Odysseus' slave. In the play, she laments the injustices of war and questions the role of the gods. She manages before the play's end to exact some revenge by blinding Polymestor and killing his sons.

Hecuba was popular in the schools of later antiquity; for example, in Byzantium it was used to teach rhetoric. The Renaissance, too, was fond of this powerful story and the image of the suffering and abused Queen of Troy. One of Shakespeare's most familiar lines invokes her when Hamlet cries out: "What's Hecuba to him or he to Hecuba / That he should weep for her?" And to the First Player in that same play in his speech on Priam, she is the fabled "mobled queen." Homer mentions her, though keeps her generally in the background, but to the Athenian tragedians, in particular Euripides, she was a highly dramatic figure, whose suffering and sorrow proved riveting to fifth-century audiences.

Given the worldwide war atrocities we have come to take almost for granted on our televisions, it is not surprising that this mother of sorrow, Hecuba, is finding her way back onto our stages, as in Edward Bond's revival of her in 1978 in his indictment-of-war play, *The Woman*. The story of *Hecuba* is simple enough for a child to embrace without difficulty, yet Hecuba is as complex as any dramatic character in human motivation and character.

A Matter of Structure

Hecuba, as it happens, is a much-disputed play. Many find its structure problematic. Euripides was fond of putting together two subjects in a single play. He does it in *Alcestis* with such success that it is seamless; *Andromache* some would say is less successful. *Hecuba* and *Trojan Women* also have two potential subjects, which, according to some critics, fatally fragments these plays. The dual subject also doesn't follow the traditional structure of an Athenian tragedy. According to Aristotle, in his *Poetics*, a tragedy must not have two subjects. He much preferred unified action, such as Sophocles' *Oedipus the King*. That *Hecuba* does not follow the traditional structure of a tragedy according to Aristotle has definitely influenced how people have viewed the play over the past two hundred years.

The "fragmentation" of *Hecuba* has almost equally divided critics. Some reject it as a failure because it's disjointed. Others go to great lengths to show that it is not fragmented but sewn together in almost every possible way, although subtly. David Kovacs takes up a refreshing standpoint when he writes: "It may be, however, that we should simply accept the fact that two stories have been put in the same play to variegate and enrich the theme of Hecuba's fall into misery."

ELECTRA

That first scene of *Electra* must have caused quite a stir on that day somewhere around 420 when the audience gathered in the Theater of Dionysus at Athens for the first performance. What was on that stage? Certainly not the expected façade of the royal palace at Mycenae, the former home of the slain Agamemnon in Argos. Instead, they saw a rude mountain cottage overlooking the valley of Argos, with the swift Inachos flowing through it. And who should emerge from the cottage to address those 20,000 or so male Athenian citizens? Of all people, a farmer! What could have been in Euripides' mind, they must have thought. Well, the newcomers, at least, would have wondered. But by this time, most theatergoers were fairly used to the idiosyncrasies of the unpredictable Euripides. He was, after all, past sixty.

In the opening prologue, some fifty-three lines long (in the Greek), this farmer addresses the audience and sets the stage for what is to come. We learn that the scene is Argos, and that it was from here that Agamemnon set sail with a thousand ships for Troy. It's obvious now that we're being given background information to set up the story to come. The farmer doesn't dawdle. Within a line or two, Priam is dead, Troy is in ruins, and Agamemnon killed on his return by his wife, Clytemnestra, and her lover, Aegisthus. Clytemnestra and Aegisthus now sit on his throne.

The farmer then tells us about Electra and Orestes, the children of Agamemnon and Clytemnestra. Aegisthus, concerned that Orestes would eventually retaliate for his father's death, was about to kill him when Agamemnon's old Tutor saved Orestes and took him to safety in Phocis. Electra, too, he wanted to kill when she reached marrying age. Her children, by a highborn husband, might also, along with Orestes, seek revenge. Clytemnestra, however, cruel as she was, stopped him. She had a reason for killing her husband, she says, but none to kill her children.

Aegisthus then devised an alternate plan. He offered a reward to any man who killed Orestes, and he married off Electra to a nobody. That nobody is, of course, the farmer. The farmer is quick to say that he's of good stock, though poor, and as a sign of his sense of honor, this gentle farmer informs us that he has never entered Electra's bed, that she is still a virgin. "I would be shamed," he says, "of my lack of worthiness to force so great an outrage on a daughter of the royal house." Besides, what would he say to Orestes, should he ever return, when he becomes aware of her poor marriage? He ends his prologue by saying that anyone who calls him a fool for not touching his own wife "measures modesty by the faulty standard of his own character." At which point the farmer goes around to the rear of the cottage to fetch a tool, and Electra enters.

Conventionally — as in Aeschylus' *Oresteia* and in Sophocles' *Electra* — plays about Electra take place in front of the palace of Agamemnon at Mycenae. It has become a house of horrors by virtue of Agamemnon's and Cassandra's murders, not to mention the anticipated deaths of Clytemnestra and Aegisthus. But in place of the traditional scene of horror, we have in Euripides a pleasant country mountainside. This scene of rural natural beauty will later become the setting for a series of atrocities that, ironically, are far from natural.

Seeing Electra Anew

Euripides' choice of setting allows him to show a side of Electra that neither Aeschylus nor Sophocles show. In Aeschylus' *Libation Bearers* and in Sophocles' *Electra*, Electra is forced by Aegisthus to live in deprivation in the palace. But in Euripides the pain and deprivation she suffers is for the most part self-imposed. Her opening speech, as she enters from the cottage with a water jar balanced on her head, lays out for us the program of her misery, which we will hear about from her to the end:

Night, black night, nurse of the golden stars, wrapped in your somber mantle I carry this jar to fetch water from the spring. No, it's not that I am forced by Necessity to carry out such tasks. I want only to show the gods how vilely Aigisthos treats me, and to cry out to the broad vault of the sky my grief for my father in his grave. My mother, that accursed descendant of Tyndareos, to please her new husband, has thrown me out, tossed me from my home. She sleeps in his bed, she bears him children, while Orestes and I are cast out as bastard offspring.

Electra's first appearance is in the guise of a slave, and "guise" is precisely the word, for, as we will soon learn, she has chosen it; it is part of the role she is playing. Why a slave, when, despite her humble circumstances, the household has its own slaves to do the work? But here she is, before dawn, with a water jar on her head, about to go off to the spring to fetch water. She lets us know that she doesn't do this out of necessity; she wants to demonstrate to the gods how badly Aegisthus is treating her. But along with the gods, she's equally, if not more, interested in making a show for the world at large (or as much of it as is at her disposal: the local village) of her misery and suffering.

She complains that her mother, Clytemnestra, "that accursed descendant of Tyndareos," has thrown her out, tossed her from her rightful home in the palace. What Electra fails to mention is that Aegisthus' original plan was to kill her, and that Clytemnestra intervened and saved her. She ends her opening speech by berating her mother for sleeping in Aegisthus' bed and for bearing him children while she and Orestes are cast out as "bastard offspring."

Something is missing here. According to the original myth, Electra's entire life is centered around her grief for her father. But Euripides' Electra laments more for herself than for her beloved father. Out of ten lines (in the Greek), she refers to her father only once in one line, whereas *I*, *me*, and *my* are repeated a total of ten times. This contrasts sharply with Electra's opening speech in

Aeschylus' *Libation Bearers*. In that speech, she directs all her thoughts and words to her father, the sole concern of her life. The same is true for her opening speech in Sophocles. After her invocation to "holy light . . . oh air embracing the earth's broad frame," so different from her invocation in Euripides, she thinks of nothing but her slaughtered father. Euripides' heroine has an entirely different agenda from her counterparts in Aeschylus and Sophocles.

As if to confirm Electra's conscious intent to suffer, Euripides has the farmer reenter to meet his wife on her way to fetch water. He is a gentle man and is troubled that she is putting herself in such a demeaning position; he's told her this before, but she continues to do the task. Her reason, if we can believe her, is to help lighten his load, but we suspect an ulterior motive. He accepts her desire to do the task and ends with the thought, "the spring's not far," and we see Euripides behind the line saying, in effect, *after all, it's not that big a task.*

Upon her return from the spring, Electra sings fifty-four lines (in the Greek) about her misery, the bitter tears she weeps. Just as before, all but a few lines are devoted to herself. She mentions Agamemnon early on, but it is really a reference to herself as Agamemnon's child, she who is "known now, known to all, as wretched Electra, wretched, pitiful Electra!" Then a few lines about Agamemnon lying "in death's dark grip," and back again to her and her misery. Virtually every mention of Agamemnon ends with her lamenting *her* pain and sorrows. Euripides uses every opportunity to show how his heroine revels in self-martyrdom.

A New Take on Orestes as Well

If Euripides' Electra differs radically from her portrayal in Aeschylus and Sophocles, so, too, does his Orestes. In Aeschylus and Sophocles, Orestes and his friend Pylades appear in front of the royal palace, well prepared for what may come. They are boldly aggressive and ready for a fight.

But Euripides' Orestes appears in the countryside outside Mycenae. Orestes, the heroic figure of Greek myth, here enters Argos by stealth. He says, "I thought it best not to enter the city walls for fear of being detected, and so have kept close here to the border for two reasons. To be able to escape quickly to a safer country if spotted by the king's henchmen, and then to find my sister. Rumor has it she's married now." This Orestes is a far cry from Aeschylus' self-assured returning hero, standing at the very gates of his father's palace. Sophocles' Orestes is equally self-assured. He enters with Pylades and his old Tutor and immediately sets to work, even before Electra's appearance. He has everything planned out in advance, even down to the deceptive "tale" the Tutor will tell of Orestes' "death" at Delphi. When Sophocles' Orestes leaves, we have no doubt that he has the situation in hand.

By contrast, Euripides' Orestes arrives with no plans and is relying on first finding his sister and devising a plan with her. "When I find her," he says, "we'll plan and carry out the murders together."

Euripides, with his uncertain Orestes and self-centered Electra, was giving his audience what it most delighted in: variations on a mythic theme, highly theatrical twists and turns leading down a previously untrodden path.

TROJAN WOMEN

The year of *Trojan Women*, 415, is one of the few secure dates in the canon of Euripides' extant plays. It was listed as winning second prize at the City Dionysia in Athens. It is also the last year of an uneasy six-year truce, begun in 421, in the Peloponnesian War: Athens was still, technically speaking, at peace. But peace or no peace, Euripides, by the time he wrote *Trojan Women* in 415, had seen enough horrors to determine that, in particular regarding prisoners of war, both Athens and its enemies were guilty of atrocities.

The cruel fate of war prisoners is recorded in Thucydides. In 431, even before war had been declared between Sparta and Athens, a party of more than three hundred Thebans, working with a group of Plataean traitors, attempted to seize Plataea, a nearby city and an ally of Athens. The operation failed. The Thebans surrendered, assuming their lives would be spared. They were, however, executed, all 180 of them. Four years into the war, in 427, Plataea surrendered to the Spartans and Thebans. Its defense force of more than two hundred was executed along with twenty-five Athenians who had been with them in the siege. "The women were made slaves," writes Thucydides. "As for the city . . . they razed it to the ground from its very foundations . . ." In the same year, Athens put down revolts in several cities on Lesbos Island, its ally, in particular Mytilene. Athens voted to punish Mytilene by executing all the men of military age and enslaving all the women and children. Shortly after the ship was dispatched to Lesbos, Athens changed its mind. Immediately, another ship was sent to intercept the first. The men rowed nonstop to catch up with the first and arrived just in time to prevent the massacre.

In the summer of 421, Athens recaptured Skione, an ally city in northern Greece that had revolted. "They put to death," writes Thucydides, "the men of military age, made slaves of the women and children, and gave the land to the Plataeans to live on." The Spartans were no better. In the winter of 417, they marched against Argos and in the process "took the Argive town of Hysia, putting to death all the free men who fell into their hands."

And then there was Melos, a city on a small island in the southern Aegean. Melos had helped Athens win the battle of Marathon in 490 by contributing ships. But it had remained neutral ever since, which angered Athens. In 415, Athens sent out an expedition to Melos. They laid siege to the city, put all military age men to death, and sold everyone else into slavery.

Was the slaughter at Melos on Euripides' mind when he wrote *Trojan Women?* For a long time, scholars have assumed it was. But it is now believed that the author didn't have time to write the play between the time of the incident at Melos and the early March production of *Trojan Women* in Athens. There were plenty of other examples, however, of captured populations being treated brutally. And even if Melos wasn't on Euripides' mind as he wrote his play, Melos was unquestionably on the minds of the Athenian spectators in the Theater of Dionysus in 415.

Down-to-Earth Characterization

Trojan Women is unique in its form and content among not only Euripides' plays but among all existing Athenian tragedies. Many have complained about Euripides' tendency to write episodic plays: *Trojan Women* is broken down into four or five scenes (depending on where the breaks are made). However, the character of Hecuba, who is onstage throughout, unites the play. Also, the time frame of the action is very narrow, the succession of scenes seems inevitable, and the plot is less intricate than many of Euripides' other plays. Most of the characters in the play are women who are essentially ordinary people caught up in extraordinary circumstances. The characters of Hecuba and Andromache are far more normal and accessible than Euripides' other female characters, such as Electra, Medea, or Phaedra. The feelings they have for their children, grandchildren, husbands, and parents are like those of millions of people for their families. Unlike many of Euripides' other tragedies, the cruelty that strikes them comes from the outside, and not from some inner neurosis or pathological condition. They are not passive victims but active and real in their reactions. They offer hope and are a tribute to the human spirit in the face of tragedy.

But no tribute, one might say, to the Greeks. The Athenians and Spartans alike imposed precisely such cruelties on enemies and former allies during the progress of this nearly thirty-year war. The cruelties at Mytilene, Skione, Hysia, and Melos had occurred only months earlier for those Athenian male citizens sitting in the Theater of Dionysus at Athens on that March day.

ORESTES
The Play as a Historical Reflection

At the close of the fifth century, democratic Athens was the scene of several oligarchic revolutions, one example being the Four Hundred who took over and ruled Athens in 411. In a Greek democracy, political rights were extended to all adult males in the "nonimmigrant population." There were practically no limitations in eligibility for holding office for these male citizens. But in an oligarchy, some free adult male citizens were excluded from even basic political rights, and even more might be excluded from holding office. In effect, then, democracy allowed the poor to be politically active; oligarchy did not. Aristotle was inspired to say that "oligarchy is the rule of the rich and democracy is the rule of the poor."

By altering the myth of Orestes, Euripides records that short-lived experience of oligarchy in 411. In the traditional handling of the myth, as in Aeschylus' *Oresteia*, or even Euripides' own *Electra*, Orestes is immediately attacked by the vengeful Furies for his murder of his mother, Clytemnestra. He goes to Delphi for cleansing by Apollo. It isn't enough. The Furies pursue him throughout Greece. Finally, Apollo directs him to Athens. There he is acquitted by Athena at the court of the Areopagus.

In *Orestes*, Euripides places the murder of Clytemnestra six days in the past. Orestes has not fled. He is seen at the play's opening feverish and hallucinating, stretched out on a bed in front of the palace, tended by a distraught Electra. Contrary to Aeschylus and other handlers of the traditional myth, including Euripides in his *Electra*, the Argive Assembly in *Orestes* is not jubilant at the end of the oppressive reign of Clytemnestra and Aegisthus. Rather, it rises violently against the two aristocratic children of the house of Agamemnon. The assembly members intend to condemn them to death for their crime and for the pollution they have brought on the city.

Euripides created his play out of events he had recently experienced. The Old Man in *Orestes*, who just happens to be passing through town on his way from the country, observes the demos of the Argive Assembly. We must assume that it was much like what Euripides saw playing itself out at similar assembly meetings on the Athenian Pnyx, the central hill in Athens, in 411. The Old Man addresses Electra:

> [When] every seat in the Assembly was filled, . . . a herald rose up and asked: "Who will speak to the issue: is Orestes to be put to death for matricide?" Up sprang Talthybios, the same who helped sack Troy with your father. A toady of a man, never know what he thinks, talks out of both sides of his mouth at once, always bowing to the first in power. He praises your father with high-flown phrases and then twists them round filthy criticism of your brother. And for what? Orestes, says he, set an example dangerous for parents. And all the while he smiles brightly at the friends of Aigisthos. But they're like that, heralds, all of them; jumping the fence, this side and that, whichever side holds the greatest power. Next came Lord Diomedes, advising not to kill you or your brother, but to satisfy religion by exile. His speech raised rounds of approval, but also disapproval. And then there arose a man whose mouth never rested. An arrogant, self-assured sort; a hireling if ever there was one. He spoke in favor of death by stoning for you and Orestes; but in truth he was nothing but a mouthpiece for Tyndareos. Another stood up then to argue the opposite. No great beauty, this man, but a man all the same, seldom seen in the town or marketplace, a small landholder, one of those we count on for the land's survival, shrewd, intelligent, a man eager to come to grips with the arguments. A man of discipline and free of corruption, whose life is above reproach. He

argued for rewarding Orestes, son of Agamemnon, he said, wreathing his head with a garland, he said, for avenging his father's murder by killing that whore of a godless wife; that woman who was depriving us of all that, of taking up arms, of going off to war, if the men who stayed behind would under-mine their houses and families by seducing the soldiers' wives. Those who were decent, at least, found him convincing, but no one spoke in support after that. Your brother then came forward, but his words, however eloquent, had no effect. The scoundrel won, the hireling, he got the most hands, the one who urged your and your brother's death. Poor Orestes had all he could do to persuade them not to kill you by stoning. And he only won that point by saying that the two of you would kill yourselves before the day's end.

The demoralized populace of Greece was as badly off in 431 according to Thucydides. Imagine the moral state of Athens after twenty-three years of warfare.

A Play That Defies Expectation

Orestes has elicited contradictory responses from critics. In its time, it was a famous and well-liked play and performed often, but since then it has become an unpopular and neglected play. Like many of Euripides' plays, this one violates standard notions of the well-constructed Greek tragedy. William Arrowsmith, in the *Tulane Drama Review*, describes the play as "[t]ragic in tone, melodramatic in incident and technique, by sudden wrenching turns savage, tender, grotesque, and even comic, combining sheer theatrical virtuosity with puzzling structural violence and a swamping bitterness of spirit. . . . [I]ts very 'queerness' and bravura of bitterness have seemed to violate both the idea of tragedy and tragic dignity itself."

Euripides wrote the play in 408 BCE, just a year before he went into voluntary exile in Macedonia. The play represents the political climate and state of affairs in Athens at that time. Arrowsmith further suggests that the play prophesizes the defeat of Athens in 404. In the final scenes of the play, there is a complete breakdown of family and social bonds. Orestes and Electra, in an attempt to avoid execution, plot with Pylades to kill Helen. When that fails, they threaten Hermione with death, and Electra threatens to burn the house down. The play, according to Arrowsmith, suggests the encroaching chaos and destruction of Athens.

In terms of insanity and criminality, Euripides' play parallels the world of the early twenty-first century and mirrors our own absurdity. Perhaps it's time for *Orestes* to be back in style and on our stages again.

BACCHAE

Although most Athenian tragedies are based on myth, the source of *Bacchae* is historical. It comes from the distant Bronze Age, well before the year 1000 BCE. It concerns the introduction of the religious rites of Dionysus into mainland Greece, most likely from Asia Minor. David Kovacs points out that we know very little about Dionysus in the Classical period and earlier. We do know from the Linear B tablets that worship of Dionysus extends back at least to the Bronze Age palace civilization of Mycenae and Pylos, which generated the tablets. Kovacs reports that this religion was centered on experiencing ecstatic union with the god Dionysus. The cult rituals of Dionysus provided a release from conventional behavior, particularly for women, who lived very circumscribed lives. The cultivation of wine is attributed to Dionysus, and he is associated with its liberating effects.

Dionysus and the Totality of Nature

In Euripides' play, wine is venerated, and even the ancient prophet Tiresias praises the glory of the god's gift. "Human kind, young man," he says to the defiant young King Pentheus, who stubbornly refuses to acknowledge that Dionysus, as a god, "has two great powers."

> First, the goddess Demeter, or whatever you may call her, earth, perhaps, our source of solid food. And then this god, *this* god, this Dionysus, son of Semele. He came later but he matched her gift when he invented for us the clear liquid juice of the grape. When we've drunk our fill, it brings an end to sorrow, brings sleep that drowns the day's cares and worries, the sole, the only remedy for our distress. Himself a god, he is poured in honor to the gods, to bring mankind their blessings. . . . Welcome this god to Thebes. Pour out wine in his honor. Wreathe your head with garlands and dance the Bakkhic dance.

To the Classical Greek, Dionysus was not exclusively, or even primarily, the god of wine. He was also called the Power in the Tree, the Blossom Bringer, the Fruit Bringer, and the Abundance of Life. According to Plutarch, the realm of Dionysus is the totality of nature: "not only the liquid fire in the grape, but the sap thrusting in a young tree, the blood pounding in the veins of a young animal, all the mysterious and uncontrollable tides that ebb and flow in the life of nature."

Oneness with the God

Wine, however, is not the only way for the follower of Dionysus to achieve personal oneness with the god, nor the most important. The Herdsman's description of the celebrating women in the clefts of Cithaeron makes that very clear: "One of them seizes a wand and strikes a rock: an icy stream leaps out. Another plunges her wand into the earth: up springs Bacchus in a flood of wine. Those eager for milk scratch the ground with their fingers: milk streams out. And pure honey spurts from the head of their wands!"

King Pentheus sees the religion as debauched and corrupt and assumes the women worshippers of Dionysus are engaged in drunken sexual revelries. The Herdsman tries to point out to Pentheus that the ritualistic wine drinking does not necessarily lead to loose behavior and describes the effect of the wine on the women:

> They were fast asleep, lying where exhaustion had dropped
> them; some leaning back against pine boughs, others resting
> their heads on pillows of oak leaves on the forest floor.
> Carelessly, perhaps, but modestly. Wine, yes, but not drunk,
> not as you say, sir, not driven to frenzy by shrieking flutes,
> not searching for sex on the mountain.

Dance, too, is a means to becoming *entheos* — one with the deity — as the chorus of Asian Bacchae sing about at length during their entry song.

Union of Opposites

It is futile, perhaps, to determine the meaning of this greatest of Athenian tragedies. Read enough of the critics and you will, sooner or later, find an interpretation that suits you — at least for a time. This play changes each time you read it; as you change, so changes the play. It demands repeated reading throughout a lifetime.

Dionysus, as noted earlier, is a composite or union of opposites. He is what any situation requires him to be. But above all else, he is a force to be reckoned with, not subordinated or ignored. He is the id, but he is also the superego, both sides of the proverbial coin. He and Pentheus are opposites, in opposition: Pentheus, the young King of Thebes, opposes the cult of Dionysus and has banned worship of Dionysus throughout Thebes. Pentheus signifies the arrogant tyrant, law and order, whereas Dionysus is all unbridled joy and revelry. And yet Dionysus and Pentheus are blood relations, cousins, both of them Theban.

The two wise old men of Thebes, Cadmus and Tiresias, try to warn the hotheaded and inexperienced boy-king that some things are better taken on faith, not fought against. They recognize the power and importance of Dionysus and dance with him on the mountain. But Pentheus fails to take their advice and becomes a victim of his arrogance: His refusal to acknowledge the god leads to his violent death, torn apart by his own mother and other female followers of Dionysus.

FINAL YEARS

In 408, when Euripides left Athens, he was in his early seventies. King Archelaus invited Euripides to Macedonia, a vast region in the north of Greece. As part of his Hellenizing policy, the king was sponsoring various Greek artists, sculptors, philosophers, and poets. For Euripides, this was a self-imposed, voluntary exile. He left Athens an embittered man, depressed over the course of the Peloponnesian War and the decline of his beloved city. He had watched it reduced to near chaos over the decades, which he had warned against repeatedly in his work. Euripides lived for two more years and died there in 406. His death mirrored the death of Pentheus in his last play, the *Bacchae*: He was accidentally attacked (some say deliberately) by the king's hunting dogs while walking in the woods and was torn to pieces.

His son (or nephew), Euripides the Younger, discovered among his effects three plays written while he lived in Macedonia. We still have the *Bacchae* and *Iphigenia in Aulis*. *Alcmaeon at Corinth* is lost. Euripides the Younger took them back to Athens and produced them, most likely in 405, at the City Dionysia. They won the coveted first prize.

DRAMATIC MOMENTS

from the Major Plays

These short excerpts are from the playwright's major plays. They give a taste of the work of the playwright. Each has a short introduction in brackets that helps the reader understand the context of the excerpt. The excerpts, which are in chronological order, illustrate the main themes mentioned in the In an Hour essay.

from **ALCESTIS** (438 BCE)

CHARACTERS

> First Old Man
> Pheres (Pherês)
> Admetus (Admêtos)

[Apollo argues with Death on the fate of Admetus and Alcestis to open the play. Then humans take their place. Admetus and his father, Pheres, debate who is responsible for the death of Alcestis, and the debate is bitter.]

Outside the palace of King Admêtos.

FIRST OLD MAN: Admêtos, look! Your father! And slaves carrying funeral gifts. How old he looks. His legs can scarcely carry him.

PHERÊS: Son, I have come to share your grief. The loss of a wise and noble wife is a dreadful blow, but one you must bear, however cruel. Accept these tokens, this finery and riches, and let them accompany her to the world below. It is only right that we honor this woman, my boy. She offered her life to save yours, and in doing so rescued me from childlessness and suffering my old age without you, my one, my only son. Her bravery has honored her sex as no woman ever has. Bless you, dear lady, dear Alkêstis, dear son's wife! You saved his life, as you did mine when my house was a desperate place. Farewell! May all go well with you in Hades' realm. (*To ADMÊTOS.*) Just between us, son, marriages like yours are rare. Most of us have no profit at all of marriage. Yours struck pure gold.

ADMÊTOS: What right have you to be here? Were you invited? By her? By me? No! You come here, you claim, as a friend, to share my grief. Friend? That's news to me! All you are is words, words without deeds! Take back your finery, your riches, what good are they to her? Her burial needs nothing of yours, and least of all you. The time to share my grief was when I was dying, when destruction threatened. But, no, you had other things in mind, and so your burden was shoved off on another, a stranger, a woman! A doddering, selfish old man would be saved by the offer of a young and vibrant life! And now you have the gall to come here to mourn her! You call yourself my father, and that woman who bore me my mother; but you were never father and mother to me. Some slave gave birth to a bastard that was smuggled into your house and given your barren sow wife's breast to suck! So much for your parentage! You were put to the test and you showed the mettle you were made of. A coward! Not my father! But a model of cowardice, who in the dying days of his doddering senility hadn't the balls to die for his own son, but let this woman, no blood relation, take your place in the grave! Shame on you! There lies the only father and mother I ever had. On that bier. Dead because you didn't give a damn. What a conquest to overcome that obstacle of cowardice that was! You should have fought to die for your son. You were old. You were decrepit. Barely able to stand; and so short on years they couldn't be counted. What would it have cost you? Everything, everything a man needs to be happy, you had. You inherited a throne and spent the best years of your life as king. You had a son, me, to succeed you and save your royal house being torn apart by other hands. And don't say I neglected or dishonored you in your old age and that's why you abandoned me. I never showed you anything but respect. And this is how you repay me, you and my mother. So if I were you, I'd rush on home and pump that sow of yours full of spare brats to tend to you in your senility, because as far as you're concerned, I'm dead. I won't be there when you die; I won't be there to dress and lay out your body for burial and have the body carried out; I'll have nothing to do with your burial! If I still live and breathe in the light of day, it's because I found another savior to give me life, and it is that person's son I am, that person, and it is to that person I pledge support in her old age! God, how I despise these old fools! They totter around on palsied feet, muttering in self-pity on the ravages of age, the desperate indignities and humiliations of the slow, tedious crawl to the grave, but let death come anywhere near, they're hale and chipper, and life's not so bad after all.

FIRST OLD MAN: Stop this, both of you. Haven't we enough sorrow as it is? Son, why exasperate your father?

PHERÊS: Who exactly do you think you're talking to, boy? Some groveling toady of an Asian slave you hauled in here from the colonies, paid for out of your private purse? I'm a Thessalian, freeborn, of a freeborn Thessalian father, a prince of Thessaly. And you and your insults go a bit far. I'm not about to be bullied by an insolent child! (*ADMÊTOS tries to interrupt.*) No, you listen to me! Don't interrupt! You attacked me, now it's your turn! By god, boy, I gave you everything I had to give. I gave you life, raised you, made you master of this house. But I did not inherit as custom from my father, nor is there in Greece, anywhere, a law that lays down that a father must die for a son. A man is born to whatever he is born to; his fate is his own, for good or ill. You have had from me everything that justice and the law require. I gave you my throne, my kingdom, you rule over a great many people, and you will receive from me at my death vast acres of land that I received from my father. So what have I left undone? What have I held back? What more do I owe you? Life? No! Don't you die for me and I won't die for you. I can see you love the light. But so do I. Or do you think, as your father, I should not? I think of the time we will spend in the Underworld and see it to be long. I look at life, and I see it to be short. Short but sweet. And then I look at you and I see one who has fought like a demon to stay alive at any cost, and, as it happens, the cost just happened to be her life. It was you who killed her, son. You! Bested by a woman in bravery! What a thing to boast of! And you call me a coward? You, the consummate coward of all. She died to save you. You! You her splendid young husband! Why, boy, you've found the fountain of youth! A foolproof road to immortality: simply convince the latest of your wives, in an endless string of them, to die in your place.

And you have the gall, you, you arrogant pretender, to accuse your own family of failing to do what to you is their duty, when you yourself are the lowest coward of all!

ADMÊTOS: I've heard quite —

PHERÊS: No, boy, you've only begun to hear! So hear a bit more! You say you love life. Well, then, let me assure you, so has everyone who ever lived. So go on, rage against us all you like. But just remember, worse things will be said of you, and they will all be true.

FIRST OLD MAN: Too many ugly words have been spoken here. Old man, stop provoking your son.

ADMÊTOS: Talk all you like. I've made my accusation, and it stands. If you find the truth painful, you shouldn't have wronged me in the first place.

PHERÊS: I'd have been even more wrong if I'd died for you.

ADMÊTOS: Is death the same for a young man as an old?

PHERÊS: We have only one life to live, not two.

ADMÊTOS: In that case, have a longer life than Zeus!

PHERÊS: Why curse your father when he's done you no wrong?

ADMÊTOS: Yes, when I see you hoarding your minutes like a miser.

PHERÊS: A miser? Tell me, then, who killed this girl?

ADMÊTOS: This dead girl is proof of your evil cowardice!

PHERÊS: It was you who took her life; you killed her.

ADMÊTOS: Oh how I hope someday you need my help!

PHERÊS: Marry a stable of wives; they can all die for you!

ADMÊTOS: That's where you're guilty! You refused to die!

PHERÊS: God's daylight is sweet; nothing sweeter.

ADMÊTOS: You have the heart of a coward, not a man.

PHERÊS: At least you're deprived of mocking your old father's burial.

ADMÊTOS: You'll die one day, too, and you will die infamous!

PHERÊS: Well, I don't think I'll let that trouble me now.

ADMÊTOS: God, the shameless cowards old men are!

PHERÊS: Was she shameless? No. Only stupid.

ADMÊTOS: Get out of here! Let me bury my dead in peace!

PHERÊS: Yes, I think we'll go. Let's let the murderer bury his victim in peace.

(PHERÊS and his SLAVES carrying the gifts begin their exit.)

ADMÊTOS: Go and good riddance! Go back to that sow wife of yours, childless old fossils, and grow older than time! You will never again be seen in my house! If I could renounce you as parents in the marketplace, I'd do it! (*To the FIRST OLD MAN.*) But come. Let's embrace the sorrow at hand, and bury our dead.

****

from **MEDEA** (431 BCE)

CHARACTERS

Medea (Mêdeia)

[Medea and her children have been abandoned by Jason, her husband, who has married another woman. He is gone. Medea is raging, and others fear what she might undertake. Her speech here is an indictment of the treatment of women. This speech ends with a plea for solidarity with the women of Corinth as she seeks retribution. For her, the battle of the sexes has become an urgent search for justice, always a Greek concern and ours still.]

In front of Mêdeia's house.

MÊDEIA: Women of Korinth, I have come out here to you to avoid being thought unfriendly. I know that both in private and in public there are conceited men, whereas others are thought indifferent to their neighbors' feelings, and for no other reason than a retiring life. Men's eyes are not to be trusted. They are unjust. Before they know a man, know his true nature, they hate the stranger, hate him on sight, having suffered no single harm. A foreigner, alien to a city's customs, must learn to live as one of its citizens, adopt its ways, its laws. But not even a citizen should resist a city's laws out of pride or stubbornness. As for me, I stand before you a foreigner struck down by disaster. A sudden blow has destroyed my life. My heart is broken. What is there now to live for? That man I once called husband, who was everything to me, my world, my all, as he knows, is now the basest of men. Of all creatures that think and feel, we women are by far the most unfortunate. First, we are expected to buy, at exorbitant price, a husband to lord it over our bodies — a further aggravation to the insult — and only then do we learn if we've chosen well or ill. A woman who divorces is not respectable; nor is it a woman's right to refuse marriage. Then, once she has taken up residence among strange habits and customs, a woman must be a prophet to divine how to deal with the guest to her bed, for at home she learned nothing. And if we are clever and manage well, and the husband is not too galled with the yoke of sex, our lives may be deemed enviable. Otherwise there is always death to look forward to. When a man grows weary of his wife and household, he can always relieve his disgust in some male friend's companionship, while we feed off one man only. Men tell us our lives are lived safely at home, while they go off to war to fight with spears. How wrong they are! I'd rather stand three times in the line of battle than bear one child! But our stories are not the same. There's no comparison. None. You have a city. You have a father's house. You have a life you can take delight in. Friends to give pleasure. But I have nothing. No relatives, no country. Only a husband who treats me like an animal, having brought me home as booty from a foreign land. I have no mother, no brother, no kinsmen, no one to give me refuge from the storms of misfortune. I ask only one thing of you, one small favor. If I light upon any means of punishing my husband for his cruelty to me, keep my secret in silence. In all things else, woman is a timorous creature, who shrinks from the sight of steel and violence. But let her be wronged in love, there is no mind more murderous.

****

from **HIPPOLYTUS** (428 BCE)

CHARACTERS

Aphrodite (Aphroditê)

[Euripides takes up a familiar theme. We are in the hands of the gods, and we defy them at our peril, for they are very much like us. So, Aphrodite explains the whole plot of the play and announces that the events she has set up are about to begin. The modern playgoer has no difficulty feeling the driving power of these subjects — sex, passion, love, desire.]

Troizen. Morning. Before the Royal Palace. Statues of Aphroditê and Artemis at either side. Enter APHRODITÊ.

APHRODITÊ: Sex. Passion. Love. Desire. These are the powers that make me the goddess I am, able to lure men to the ends of the earth. I make fools of some along the way, but am honored by most, even by the gods, who are not above thrashing about in my sweet snares. My name is Aphroditê. Those who don't fight my compulsions, I reward in the most wonderful of ways. Compulsions? Say, rather, to be honest, idiosyncrasies, notions, impulses, whims. But put in my path a man too proud to play my game, too arrogant, too haughty to do me reverence, and I will see to it that he pays with his life for his foolishness. We gods are no different from you. We all love it when men pay us court. Listen, now; I'll prove the truth of my words. There's a man here in Troizen, the bastard son of Thêseus, king of Athens and Troizen, and his sometime Amazon woman. His name? Hippolytos. A lover of the hunt as of horses. But Hippolytos being a bastard, his father sent him here to his grandfather Pittheus to raise, and eventually to become king of Troizen. Better to keep him out of Athens than stir up unwanted rivalry with the legal offspring. Now. This Hippolytos is a real thorn in my side. He simply cannot stomach what I stand for and hates me with a passion that borders on the manic. And the thought of love or marriage drives him insane. And sex! Oh god! Sex is no happy word on his lips! It terrifies him. Instead of me, he honors Artemis, sister of Apollo and daughter of mighty Zeus. To listen to him, she's the greatest god on Olympos. No praise is too much, no honor too extravagant. They're a pair. Never apart. When he's tracking wild beasts in the forest with his hounds and men, she's there, his tutelary spirit, right beside him. A very odd relationship — mortal and divine. Currying favor, would you say, above his station? Oh, and did I mention she's a virgin? Well! But do I let it trouble me? No, why should I? And yet one thing is certain. I will repay him, this Hippolytos. He will learn not to neglect me. Unfortunately, his debt comes due no later than — today. And I haven't dawdled, take my word for it. Everything needed to pay this debt was set in motion some time ago, and now all that's needed is a little "encouragement" to bring it to a conclusion. Here's what I've managed so far. Once, on his way from Troizen, Hippolytos made his way through Athens to Eleusis to take part in the Sacred Mysteries. Now, as it happens, Thêseus and his noble wife, Phaidra, were living in Athens at the time, when Phaidra caught sight of him, the beautiful Hippolytos, and, by my scheming, was pounded with such a hammer-blow to the heart that it almost destroyed her, poor thing. She suffered so that, even before she and Thêseus came here to Troizen, Phaidra had built and dedicated to me a temple on the Akropolis. Her reason? From there she could look out across the waters, here to Troizen, and behold the land that held her distant love. A temple, I might say, that men in ages still to come will dedicate to the memory of — you've guessed it! Hippolytos. Later, Thêseus managed treacherously to kill the two sons of Pallas in a political fracas. He was asked — diplomatically of course — to leave Athens for a year of "self-exile" so as not to pollute the city with his blood-guilt. And all this time poor Phaidra was eaten away by the lust that tore her to shreds. And being a modest and proper woman, she said nothing, not a word, to anyone, she was so ashamed. In fact, she put on a silence that, if I'm any judge, is out to destroy her. Who, after all, could help her? No one. No one knows the source of her illness. But this is not what fate has in mind for poor Phaidra's passion. Now. Here's my plan. I'll expose this entire affair. To Thêseus, to everyone, to them all. They'll all know. And this will work very hard on Phaidra, poor thing, whose sense of propriety is the talk of all Athens. Once I've done this, this ravishing but arrogant young man who wars against me with all his forces — will die. The weapon? A gift that sea-god Poseidon once gave to Thêseus. A trio of curses. He'll need only one, of course, to drag the monstrous Hippolytos and his epic hatred down to his death by the sea! Ah! And then, of course, there's Phaidra! Poor Phaidra! She'll die, too. Not, of course, dishonored. She'll still have hold on her stainless reputation. I'll see to that. Still and all, she'll have to die. I mean, which is more important? Her life, or my satisfaction in exercising a proper revenge on my enemies? But here he comes now. Radiant as ever. A real heartbreaker, Hippolytos, back from the hunt with his band of pretty boys. And so I withdraw as they enter with great jubilation, singing hymns of praise to Artemis, his favorite miss. He hasn't a clue, has Hippolytos, that the gates of Hades are swinging wide to welcome him with open arms. Today's sun won't set till his life has run out. (*Exit.*)

****

from **ELECTRA** (ca. 420 BCE)

CHARACTERS

Electra (Êlektra)
Orestes (Orestês)
First Young Argive Woman

[This scene follows Electra's recognition of Orestes and their agreement to murder Aegisthus and Clytemnestra, who together killed Agamemnon, their father. The deed of revenge is completed — Orestes has murdered Aegisthus. The consequences of the deed, beginning with the outpouring of Electra's thoughts to her brother, Orestes, start to unfold. Deep questions about justice are inescapable.]

Outside a small rustic mountain cottage. Enter ORESTÊS, carrying the head of AIGISTHOS, and PYLADÊS with their MALE SLAVES, who carry the body of AIGISTHOS, then ÊLEKTRA from the cottage with two garlands.

ÊLEKTRA: Noble victor, glorious champion, Orestês, son of the father who won the prize at Troy, accept this humble garland for your head! Won not for running some futile footrace, but for victory over the enemy, Aigisthos, victory over the usurper who murdered our father! And you, Pyladês, equally deserving, comrade in arms and son of a most loyal father, accept this garland I now place on your head! Your prize in this is no less great than his. May your fortune be always blest!

ORESTÊS: The gods first, Êlektra, praise them first, for they are the makers of our good fortune, and then praise me, but with them, for I am only their servant and fortune's. I stand here the killer of Aigisthos not in word but in deed. (*Lifting the head aloft.*) And if anyone needs more proof, here is his body. Cast it out for wild beasts to tear at, or impale it on a stake and set it out for birds to peck, those children of the air. The man who was once your master is now your slave.

ÊLEKTRA: I'm so ashamed — and yet I have to speak.

ORESTÊS: Ashamed? But you have nothing to fear.

ÊLEKTRA: Blame for insulting the dead.

ORESTÊS: No one would censure you for that.

ÊLEKTRA: Our people are quick to criticize.

ORESTÊS: Sister, say whatever you like; our hatred for this man knows no bounds. (*Hands the head to ÊLEKTRA.*)

ÊLEKTRA: So then. Here we are at last. But where to begin? Not to say where to end and what in between. And all of it insult after insult, a catalogue of wrongs you did to me, to us, to us both, to Orestês and me. Morning after morning after morning, in the pale light of innumerable dawns, I have rehearsed what to say to you to your face, if ever my fear were lifted, as now it is. But I'm free now, free to make my settlement for your mistreatment, your evil acts against me that I so wanted to make while you still lived. You ruined me, you destroyed my life when you deprived me, us, me and Orestês, of our dearly loved father, for what had we done to deserve such wrong? You married, shamefully married, our mother, and killed her husband, the man who commanded the assembled Greeks at Troy, you, who never set foot inside that war. Your crassness reached such heights of stupidity that you believed, once married to my mother, you would have a virtuous wife in bed, even though she was unfaithful to my father — with you! A man who has corrupted another man's wife in secret liaison, and then is forced to take her, should know that she will be as unfaithful to him as she was to her former husband. Your life was a constant torment, and yet you pretended you lived well enough. You knew you had made a marriage that offended heaven, and our mother knew she had married a godless man. You were evil, both of you, and you each knew that you took on each other's depravity. The rumor scuttled around Argos, every tongue, that you, her man, were "Klytaimnêstra's husband," rather than she, your woman, "Aigisthos' wife." What a disgrace, for a woman to head the household! And I despise the child whose name in the city comes not from its father but its mother, for the man who makes a marriage above his station in the end counts for nothing beside the woman. Oh, and how deceived you were in thinking that wealth gave you power. But money never lasts; a brief friend that leaves as quickly as it came. It's character that lasts, not possessions. Character is a partner, a support in adversity; while wealth, ignorant of justice, resides with fools: it blossoms briefly and off it flies. As for your way with women, it's more than a virgin can say, and so I'll only hint at what I know. You with your palace and wealth of possessions, you who pranced and paraded in a king's house, primping and preening, flaunting your hard body, yes, and your beauty — the outrages you committed to sate your evil! But give me a real man anytime to a pretty-boy cipher; a man whose sons make brave soldiers. The other sort are for dancing and decorating choruses. I damn you, ignorant fool! Time has stripped you of every defense, and I only wish you knew the price you paid. A man devoted to evil must not pride himself too early in thinking that he has run well and outstripped Justice. Let him wait till he nears the goal and has run his life's last course before presuming!

FIRST YOUNG ARGIVE WOMAN: He paid horribly for his horrible deeds to you and Orestês. The might of Justice is great!

ÊLEKTRA: So then. Here we are. Slaves, carry in the body. Hide it in the shadows; when my mother comes she mustn't catch sight of the corpse before we've slaughtered her.

(*The MALE SLAVES carry the body of AIGISTHOS into the cottage. ÊLEKTRA starts to follow them, as ORESTÊS catches sight of KLYTAIMNÊSTRA's approach a long way off.*)

****

from **BACCHAE** (after 406 BCE)

CHARACTERS

Tiresias (Teiresias)
Cadmus (Kadmos)
Pentheus
First Bacchae (First Bakkhê)

[Dionysus opens the play by demanding his due as a god. Then
Tiresias, the blind seer, arrives at Thebes and calls out to his old friend
Cadmus to join him in the Bachhic revels. Cadmus joins him, also
dressed for the revels. A discussion of wise attitudes toward the gods
and religion ensues. Later they encounter Pentheus, Cadmus' grandson, who has none of these attitudes and who believes that force
should be used to quell the rites. Conflicts about women's sexuality and
how it is to be controlled loom large in Pentheus' mind. Today's playgoer has merely to look around the world to see that these issues are
still important.]

Thebes. In front of the palace of Pentheus.

TEIRESIAS: (*Enters from the side.*) Ooo-ooo! Anyone here? Anyone at
the gates? Ooo-ooo! Someone! Anyone! Where's the porter! Who's
in charge? Call him! Kadmos! Agenor's son! Call him from the
palace! That immigrant Agenor from Sidon who came to Thebes to
build her battlements. Call him! It's me. Teiresias. I'm waiting, tell
him. He'll know what for. We have a pact, we two old goats, Kadmos and I. We'll do it, we said, and now I'm here, ready to go, withered old limbs and all, dressed in fawn-skins, green ivy tied round
my wand and crowning my head.

KADMOS: (*Enters from the palace.*) Ah, old friend! I knew it! Knew it
was you! I was in the palace when I heard that voice. "That voice,"
I said to myself, "with such wisdom in it, can only be my old friend

Teiresias." But here I am, fawn-skin and all, ready to honor the god, dressed for his revels, ready to go. This god? You know? This Dionysos we're all hearing about? Well! He's my daughter's son. It's true. Yes, truly. We must help him. Everything we can. Do our part, you and I, to raise him high in men's eyes! Dionysos! Who has revealed himself to mortals! But where do we go? You're the wise one, old friend, eh? Explain to this withered old cocker, where do we go to join the god's dancers? We'll go, you and I, eh? We'll go, tossing our scraggly white manes to the winds. We'll dance all night, we'll leap, we'll whirl, turning, turning, never tiring till our feet fall off! Then all next day we'll pound, pound, pound the earth with our wands! What a joy to forget how old we are!

TEIRESIAS: Me, too, me, too! Ah, Kadmos! Kadmos! Young again! Let's dance again!

KADMOS: Time to go, don't you think? To the mountains? But what if we took a carriage? Hm?

TEIRESIAS: Carriage? Carriage? Never! No, never! That would never do! The god will demand more reverence than that, don't you know!

KADMOS: Well, old Bakkhant, then I'll have to lead the way; lead you like the ancient baby you are.

TEIRESIAS: No need, old friend, Bakkhos will do that.

KADMOS: Where are they? Where are the men? Are no other men of Thebes to dance for Dionysos?

TEIRESIAS: Men of Thebes! Ha! We're the only sane ones here! The men are mad! Stark crazy insane!

KADMOS: Then why are we wasting time? At our age what's there to waste! Here, take my hand.

TEIRESIAS: Yes, yes, I have it. There. Hold tight now. Don't want to lose this old fool, do we?

KADMOS: Fool! That's it! That's it! All fools! That's what they are, these men of Thebes! But I'm no fool. Not me. Not old Kadmos. I'm only a mortal. I don't take any god lightly.

TEIRESIAS: Right you are. Who are we to go around doubting gods?

Who exists, who doesn't? Not for me. No, no. I mean, where does that put tradition? You know? Tradition? Our fathers' beliefs, old as time? Nothing can pry those loose for me. Not even wise men, with all their crafty reasoning can ever break their hold on our lives. Leastways not that crazy grandson of yours, that Pentheus. I can just hear them now, the old stick-in-the-muds with their wooly minds, when I twine my head with ivy and go out to dance the god's dance! "Balmy old codger!" they'll say, "and at his age! Has he no shame! Vine leaves, indeed!" But this god, this, this, this Dionysos. Tell me, Kadmos, tell me, when did he say that only the young should dance? Hm? That can't be right. No. Cruel! The old, too! And why not? Why not the old, too? No, no! No god ever made such a law. What he wants, this, this Dionysos, this Bakkhos, or whatever it is he's called, he has so many! What he wants is equal honor from all. No one left out. No one. Joy! Joy is all he asks of us!

KADMOS: All right, all right, calm down. Now, I know you're blind as a bat, you old goat, so let's let me be the see-er for once, and — oh god! — tell you that I see Pentheus coming this way. In a mad rush, too, in one of his moods. Ekhion's boy, my grandson, the one I gave my powers to governing Thebes. Just a boy, but what can you do. And he's moving like a house on fire. I wonder what bee he's got in his bonnet this time?

PENTHEUS: (*Enters with GUARDS.*) What is this! I demand an answer! Now! I was out of Thebes when I heard! Some vile eruption of evil here in the city! Some insanity let loose! Our women lured from their homes! To frisk in dark nooks in mountain forests in search of fraudulent ecstasies! Dancing in honor of some upstart divinity! Some Dionysos, or whatever it is they call him! Possesses women with lewd, hypnotic spells, or so I've heard! Drinking wine from overflowing bowls! Hiding in caverns to fuck with lusting males! Sacred Maenad priestesses they call themselves! Sworn to Bakkhos, they say, but more at home with Aphroditê, if I have two wits about me! Some I've already trapped. Bound and chained in the stables. The others will be tracked down soon enough. In the mountains. Once I've locked them in irons in cages, I'll stamp out the vermin of their obscene orgies! And what's this about an intruder? Some newly arrived foreigner in the city? A wizard sorcerer from Lydia? Curls to his shoulders, golden, perfumed! Cheeks the color of wine! Love-spells of Aphroditê in his eyes! Days and nights he spends with young girls, dangling before them the obscene lure of his orgies. Get him inside these walls, he'll be done pounding his precious wand and bouncing his curls. I'll have his head, this stranger who claims Dionysos is a god! Says he's a god, does he? Sewn into Zeus' thigh? We'll see! Fact is, if anyone is interested, Dionysos was burned to a crisp along with his mother. Zeus' lightning punishment for her lie that he was her lover. A man possessed of such insolence deserves hanging. Ah! But here's another miracle! Our ancient seer Teiresias. In dappled fawn-skin, no less. And what's this? Grandfather? Grandfather Kadmos? Playing the Bakkhant? How can you do this! How can you make yourself ridiculous! Decked out with your thrashing ivy wand. Throw it away. You shame me, grandfather! Have you two lost your minds? But this is your doing, Teiresias. Not enough gods in Thebes? You need another? To augment your augurer's business? Larger fees, hm? All that's saving you now, you doddering fool, is your age. Anything else and you'd be in chains down there in the dungeon with the Bakkhai. With those who imported these disgusting rites to Thebes. When the sparkle of wine flows at women's feasts, you know there's nothing healthy in those mysteries.

FIRST BAKKHÊ: This is blasphemy, King Pentheus. You insult the gods, you insult Kadmos who sowed the dragon's teeth. You're the son of Ekhion. Are you trying to deny your race?

TEIRESIAS: Give a wise man an honest case to argue and words come easy. But your words, young man, the words that fall easy from your tongue, are neither wise nor clever. A man whose strength rests solely in his self-assurance is a bad citizen. For all his words, he's short on reason. He's a fool. This new god you ridicule? There are no words for how great his fame will be throughout all Hellas. Humankind, young man, has two great powers. First, the goddess Dêmêter, or whatever you may call her, earth, perhaps, our source of solid food. And then this god, this god, this Dionysos, son of Semelê. He came later but he matched her gift when he invented for us the clear liquid juice of the grape. When we've drunk our fill, it brings an end to sorrow, brings sleep that drowns the day's cares and worries, the sole, the only remedy for our distress. Himself a god, he is poured in honor to the gods, to bring mankind their blessings. This god is also a prophet. And frenzied Bakkhic madness inspires prophecy. When the god enters the possessed like a storm wind, they go mad, raving mad, but they see the future. And what they see comes true. And Dionysos also helps the god of War. When an army stands ranged and ready for battle, they are sometimes struck with panic fear and flee, before raising so much as a single spear. This madness, too, comes from Dionysos. But you will see him one day, with his Maenad bands, bounding over the rocks at Delphi, across the twin-peaks of Parnassos, with pine-torches, leaping, whirling, thrashing his Bakkhic wand, great in all of Greece. Listen to me, Pentheus. Don't mistake that force alone governs human affairs. And if your mind is sick, don't presume to think yourself sane. Welcome this god to Thebes. Pour out wine in his honor. Wreathe your head with garlands and dance the Bakkhic dance. As for that matter that causes you so much torment: sex. Oh my boy, Dionysos doesn't suppress lust in a woman. You must look for that in the woman herself, in her nature. Not even at the height of Bakkhic ecstasy will a chaste woman be anything less than chaste. Just think, my boy, the pleasure you take when throngs stand at the gates, magnifying the name of Pentheus. Gods, no less than kings, demand respect. And so, Kadmos and I, for all your scoffing, your insane laughter, will wreathe our heads with ivy, take up our wands, and old and gray as we are, we will dance the god's dance. Two old fools, no doubt, but dance we will, for we have no choice. No logic of yours will persuade me to fight the god. For you are mad, Pentheus, cruelly mad, and no drug can cure your sickness, though a drug must surely have caused it.

FIRST BAKKHÊ: Apollo would agree with you, old Teiresias, and you show wisdom in honoring the mighty god Bromios.

KADMOS: Teiresias advises well, my boy. Stay with us. Don't break with tradition. You're all in the air just now, lost your balance. If, as you believe, this is no god, say, at least, that he is. A pious lie that credits Semelê as mother of a god and honors the whole family. And don't forget how your cousin Aktaion died. His man-eating hounds that he himself had raised tore him to bits on the same mountain where the Bakkhai dance. He boasted he was a greater hunter than Artemis. Don't let that be you, son. Here, let me crown you with this ivy. Join us. Join us in honoring the god.

PENTHEUS: Don't touch me! Get away from me with that crown! Go play at your Bakkhanals, but don't smear your madness off onto me. Teiresias, your instructor in lunacy, will pay for this where it hurts most. Someone! Go! Go quickly! To this old fool's seat of augury. There where he ponders his birds and their droppings. Pry it up for him. Pry it up with crowbars. Heave it over. Smash it. Raze it to the ground. And when you're done, throw his sacred ribbons to the storm winds. This sacrilege will gall him to the core. The rest will patrol the city for this effeminate, this girlish stranger. He infects our women. Some new disease is afoot. It fouls our beds with his "rituals." Track him down. When you've caught him, tie him up and bring him here to me. He'll die the death he deserves. Death by stoning. He will regret having imported his orgies to Thebes. Go!

(Exeunt GUARDS in haste.)

TEIRESIAS: Poor young fool! How little you know the meaning of your words. You were out of your mind before. Now you're raving. Come, Kadmos. Let's go pray for this brutish man, and for the city, that the god will be patient with us. Come with me. You try to hold me up, as I will you. And bring your wand, the god's wand. Two old codgers like us mustn't be caught falling on their faces. What a disgrace that would be. We must go now, to serve Dionysos, son of Zeus. Ah, Kadmos, the name Pentheus means "grief." Let's pray the god brings no grief into your house. This is no prophecy, only fact. The fool speaks folly.

(Exeunt KADMOS and TEIRESIAS; then PENTHEUS into the palace.)

****

Euripides

THE READING ROOM

YOUNG ACTORS AND THEIR TEACHERS

Bieber, Margarete. *The History of the Greek and Roman Theater.* 2nd ed. Revised. Princeton, N.J.: Princeton University Press, 1961.

Bury, J. B., and Russell Meiggs. *A History of Greece to the Death of Alexander the Great.* 4th ed. Revised. New York: St. Martin's Press, 1991.

Csapo, Eric, and William J. Slater. *The Context of Ancient Drama.* Ann Arbor: The University of Michigan Press, 1995.

Finley, M. I. *The Ancient Greeks: An Introduction to Their Life and Thought.* New York: The Viking Press, 1964.

Flickinger, R. C. *The Greek Theater and Its Drama.* Chicago: University of Chicago Press, 1936.

Forrest, W. G. *The Emergence of Greek Democracy.* New York: McGraw-Hill, 1966.

Goldhill, Simon. *Reading Greek Tragedy.* Cambridge: Cambridge University Press, 1986.

Green, J. R. *Theatre in Ancient Greek Society.* London and New York: Routledge, 1994.

Kott, Jan. *The Eating of the Gods: An Interpretation of Greek Tragedy.* New York: Random House, 1973.

Ley, Graham. *A Short Introduction to the Ancient Greek Theater.* Chicago: The University of Chicago Press, 1991.

Traulos, Johannes. *Pictorial Dictionary of Ancient Athens.* London: Thames and Hudson, 1971.

Walcot, Peter. *Greek Drama in Its Theatrical and Social Context.* Cardiff: The University of Wales Press, 1976.

This extensive bibliography lists books about the playwright according to whom the books might be of interest. If you would like to research further something that interests you in the text, lists of references, sources cited, and editions used in this book are found in this section.

SCHOLARS, STUDENTS, PROFESSORS

Adkins, A. W. H. *Merit and Responsibility: A Study in Greek Values.* Oxford: Oxford University Press, 1960.

Aristotle. *The Poetics.* Translated by Gerald Else, tr. Ann Arbor: University of Michigan Press, 1967.

Arrowsmith, William A. "The Criticism of Greek Tragedy." *Tulane Drama Review* 33, 1959.

Arthur, M. "The Choral Odes of the *Bacchae* of Euripides." *Yale Classical Studies* 22, 1972.

Aylen, Leo. *The Greek Theater.* Rutherford, N.J.: Fairleigh Dickinson University Press, 1985.

Barker, Ernest. *The Politics of Aristotle.* Oxford: Oxford University Press, 1946.

Barlow, S. A. *Euripides: Trojan Women.* Warminster, UK: Aris and Phillips, 1986.

_____. *Euripides: Heracles.* Warminster, UK: Aris and Phillips, 1996.

Barrett, W. S. *Euripides: Hippolytus.* Oxford: Oxford University Press, 1964.

Bennett, Simon, M. D. *Mind and Madness in Ancient Greece.* Ithaca, N.Y.: Cornell University Press, 1978.

Blundell, Sue. *Women in Ancient Greece.* London: British Museum Press, 1995.

Boesche, Roger. *The Theories of Tyranny from Plato to Arendt.* University Park: The Pennsylvania State University Press, 1996.

Bond, G. W. *Euripides: Heracles.* Oxford: Oxford University Press, 1988.

Burian, Peter. "Euripides' *Heraclidae*: An Interpretation." *Classical Philology* 72, 1977.

_____. *New Directions in Euripidean Criticism.* Durham, N.C.: Duke University Press, 1985.

Burkert, Walter. *Greek Religion.* Cambridge: Harvard University Press, 1985.

Burnett, Anne Pippin. *Catastrophe Survived: Euripides' Plays of Mixed Reversal.* Oxford: The Clarendon Press, 1971.

_____. "Tribe and City, Custom and Decree in *Children of Heracles*." *Classical Philology* 71, 1976.

Buxton, R. G. *Persuasion in Greek Tragedy.* Cambridge: Cambridge University Press, 1982.

Collard, C. "The Funeral Oration in Euripides' *Supplices*." *Bulletin of the Institute of Classical Studies* 19, 1972.

_____. *Euripides: Hecuba*. Warminster, UK: Aris and Phillips, 1991.

Conacher, D. J. *Euripidean Drama: Myth, Theme and Structure*. Toronto and London: University of Toronto Press, 1967.

_____. *Euripides: Alcestis*. Warminster, UK: Aris and Phillips, 1988.

_____. *Euripides: Iphigenia in Aulis*. Warminster, UK: Aris and Phillips (forthcoming).

Cooper, Lane. *The Greek Genius and Its Influence*. New Haven, Conn.: Yale University Press, 1917.

Craik, E. *Euripides: The Phoenician Women*. Warminster, UK: Aris and Phillips, 1988.

Croally, N. T. *Euripidean Polemic: The Trojan Women and the Function of Tragedy*. Cambridge and New York: Cambridge University Press, 1994.

Cropp, M. *Euripides: Electra*. Warminster, UK: Aris and Phillips, 1988.

_____. *Euripides: Iphigeneia in Tauris*. Warminster, UK: Aris and Phillips, 2000.

Dale, A. M. *Euripides: Alcestis*. Oxford: Oxford University Press, 1954.

_____. *Euripides: Helen*. Oxford: Oxford University Press, 1967.

_____. *Collected Papers*. Cambridge: Cambridge University Press, 1969.

Denniston, J. D. *Euripides: Electra*. Oxford: Oxford University Press, 1939.

Detienne, Marcel. *Dionysus at Large*. Cambridge, Mass.: Harvard University Press, 1989.

Dodds, E.R. *The Greeks and the Irrational*. Berkeley and Los Angeles: University of California Press, 1951.

_____. *Euripides: Bacchae*. 2nd ed. Oxford: Oxford University Press, 1960.

_____. "Morals and Politics in the *Oresteia*" *The Ancient Concept of Progress*. Oxford: Oxford University Press, 1973.

Dunn, Francis M. *Tragedy's End: Closure and Innovation in Euripidean Drama*. Oxford: Oxford University Press, 1996.

Foley, Helene. *Ritual Irony: Poetry and Sacrifice in Euripides*. Ithaca, N.Y.: Cornell University Press, 1985.

Fontenrose, J. *The Cult and Myth of Pyrros at Delphi*. Berkeley and Los Angeles: The University of California Press, 1960.

Fugua, C. F. "The World of Myth in Euripides' *Orestes*." *Traditio* 34, 1978.

Galinsky, G. K. *The Heracles Theme.* Oxford: Oxford University Press, 1972.

Gombrich, Ernst. *Art and Illusion.* London: Phaidon, 1977.

Gredley, B. "The Place and Time of Victory: Euripides' *Medea.*" Bulletin of the Institute of Classical Studies 34, 1987.

Gregory, J. W. "Euripides' *Alcestis.*" *Hermes* 107, 1979.

Grube, G. M. A. *The Drama of Euripides.* London: Methuen, 1941.

Guthrie, W. K. C. *The Greeks and Their Gods.* London: Methuen, 1950.

Hadley, W. *Euripides: Hecuba.* Cambridge, Cambridge University Press, 1894.

Hall, Edith. *Inventing the Barbarian: Greek Self-definition Through Tragedy.* Oxford: Oxford University Press, 1989.

_____. *The Rhesus Attributed to Euripides.* Warminster, UK: Aris and Phillips, (forthcoming).

Halleran, Michael. *Stagecraft in Euripides.* London and Sydney: Croom Helm, 1985.

_____. *Euripides: Medea.* Warminster, UK: Aris and Phillips, 1995.

Halperin, David M. *One Hundred Years of Homosexuality.* New York and London: Routledge, 1990

Headlam, C. E. S. *Euripides: Iphigenia in Aulis.* Cambridge: Cambridge University Press, 1896.

Herington, C. J. *Poetry into Drama: Early Tragedy and the Greek Poetic Tradition.* Berkeley and Los Angeles: The University of California Press, 1985.

Hornblower, Simon, and Antony Spawforth, eds. *The Oxford Classical Dictionary.* 3rd ed. Oxford: Oxford University Press, 1996.

Jaeger, Werner. *Paideia: The Ideals of Greek Culture.* 3 vols. New York: Oxford University Press, 1945.

Jones, John. *On Aristotle and Greek Tragedy.* Stanford, Calif.: Stanford University Press, 1980.

Jung, Carl Gustav, and Carl Kerényi. *Essays on a Science of Mythology: The Myth of the Divine Child and the Mysteries of Eleusis.* Bollingen Series XXII. Princeton, N.J.: Princeton University Press, 1969.

Just, Roger. *Women in Athenian Law and Life.* London and New York: Routledge, 1991.

Kannicht, Richard. *Euripides: Helena.* Heidelberg, Germany: C. Winter, 1969.

Kerényi, Carl. *Dionysos: Archetypal Image of Indestructible Life.* Princeton, N.J., and London: Princeton University Press, 1976.

Keuls, Eva C. *The Reign of the Phallus: Sexual Politics in Ancient Athens.* Berkeley and Los Angeles: The University of California Press, 1993.

Kitto, H. D. F. *Form and Meaning in Drama: A Study of Six Greek Plays and of Hamlet.* 2nd ed. London: Methuen, 1964; New York: Barnes and Noble, 1968.

_____. *Greek Tragedy: A Literary Study.* 2nd ed. New York: Doubleday, 1964; 3rd ed. London: Methuen, 1966.

_____. *Poiesis: Structure and Thought.* Berkeley and Los Angeles: The University of California Press, 1966.

_____. *Word and Action: Essays on the Ancient Theater.* Baltimore, Md., and London: The Johns Hopkins University Press, 1979.

Knox, Bernard M. "The *Hippolytus* of Euripides." *Yale Classical Studies*, 13, 1952.

_____. *The Heroic Temper.* Berkeley: The University of California Press, 1964.

_____. *Word and Action: Essays on the Ancient Theater.* Baltimore, Md.: The Johns Hopkins University Press, 1979.

Knox, B. M. W. "Euripidean Comedy." *Word and Action: Essays on the Ancient Theater.* Baltimore, Md.: The Johns Hopkins University Press, 1979.

Kolb, Frank. *Agora und Theater.* Berlin: Gebrüder Mann, 1981.

Konstan, D. "An Anthropology of Euripides' *Cyclops.*" *Ramus* 10, 1981.

Kubo, M. "The Norm of Myth: Euripides' *Electra.*" *Harvard Studies in Classical Philology* 71, 1966.

Lattimore, Richmond. *The Poetry of Greek Tragedy.* Baltimore, Md.: The Johns Hopkins University Press, 1958.

_____. "Euripides' Phaedra and Hippolytus." *Arion* 1, 1962.

_____. *The Story Patterns in Greek Tragedy.* Ann Arbor: The University of Michigan Press, 1964.

Lax, Batya Casper. *Elektra: A Gender Sensitive Study of the Plays Based on the Myth.* North Carolina and London: McFarland and Company, Inc, 1995.

Lee, K. H. *Euripides: Trojan Women.* London: St. Martin's Press, 1976.

_____. *Euripides: Ion.* Warminster, UK: Aris and Phillips, 1997.

Lesky, Albin. "On the *Heraclidae* of Euripides." *Yale Classical Studies* 25, 1977.

_____. *Greek Tragedy*. London: Ernest Benn, 1978.

_____. *Greek Tragic Poetry*. New Haven, Conn.: Yale University Press, 1983.

Lloyd, M. "The Helen Scene in Euripides' *Trojan Women*." *Classical Quarterly* 34, 1984.

_____. "Divine and Human Action in Euripides' *Ion*." *Antike und Abendland* 32, 1986.

_____. *The Agon in Euripides*. Oxford: Oxford University Press, 1992.

Lloyd-Jones, Hugh. *The Justice of Zeus*. Sather Gate Lectures, vol. 41. Berkeley and Los Angeles: The University of California Press, 1971.

March, J. R. "Euripides' *Bakchai*: A Reconsideration in the Light of Vase-Paintings." *Bulletin of the Institute of Classical Studies* 36, 1989.

Mastronarde, D. *Contact and Disunity: Some Conventions of Speech and Action on the Greek Tragic Stage*. Berkeley and Los Angeles: The University of California Press, 1979.

_____. *Euripides: Phoenissae*. Cambridge: Cambridge University Press, 1994.

Meier, Christian. *The Greek Discovery of Politics*. Cambridge, Mass.: Harvard University Press, 1993.

_____. *The Political Art of Greek Tragedy*. Baltimore, Md.: The Johns Hopkins University Press, 1993.

Meridor, R. "Hecuba's Revenge." *American Journal of Philology* 96, 1978.

Michelini, Ann Norris. *Euripides and the Tragic Tradition*. Madison: University of Wisconsin Press, 1987.

Mossman, J. *Wild Justice: A Study in Euripides'* Hecuba. Oxford: Oxford University Press, 1995.

Murray, Gilbert. *Five Stages of Greek Religion*. New York, N.Y.: Columbia University Press, 1925.

_____. *Euripides and His Age*. London: Oxford University Press, 1946.

Neumann, Erich. *The Great Mother: An Analysis of the Archetype*. 2nd ed. Bollingen Series XLVII. New York: Pantheon Books, 1963.

_____. *The Origins and History of Consciousness*. 2nd printing, corrected and amended. Bollingen Series XVII. New York: Pantheon Books, 1964.

Nicklin, T. *Euripides: Supplices*. Oxford: Oxford University Press, 1936.

Nietzsche, Friedrich. *The Birth of Tragedy and Other Writings.* Cambridge Texts in the History of Philosophy. Cambridge: Cambridge University Press, 1999.

Nussbaum, Martha. *The Fragility of Goodness: Luck and Ethics in Greek Tragedy and Philosophy.* Cambridge, Mass.: Harvard University Press, 1986.

Otto, Walter. *Dionysus, Myth and Cult.* Bloomington: University of Indiana Press, 1965.

Owen, A. S. *Euripides: Ion.* Oxford: Oxford University Press, 1939.

Page, Denys L. *Actors' Interpolations in Greek Tragedy.* Oxford: The Clarendon Press, 1934.

_____. *Euripides: Medea.* Oxford: Oxford University Press, 1938.

Pearson, A. C. *Euripides: Children of Heracles.* Cambridge: Cambridge University Press, 1907.

Platnauer, M. *Euripides: Iphigenia in Tauris.* Oxford: Oxford University Press, 1938.

Podlecki, A. "Some Themes in Euripides' *Phoenissae.*" *Transaction of the American Philological Association* 93, 1962.

Pomeroy, S. *Goddesses, Whores, Wives, and Slaves: Women in Classical Antiquity.* New York: Shocken, 1995.

Porter, W. H. *The Rhesus of Euripides.* 2nd ed. Cambridge: Cambridge University Press, 1929.

Powell, Anton, ed. *Euripides, Women, and Sexuality.* London and New York: Routledge, 1990.

Pucci, P. *The Violence of Pity in Euripides' Medea.* Ithaca, N.Y.: Cornell University Press, 1980.

Rabinowitz, N. S. *Anxiety Veiled: Euripides and the Traffic in Women.* Ithaca, N.Y.: Cornell University Press, 1993.

Reckford, K. "Medea's First Exit." *Transaction of the American Philological Association* 99, 1968.

Ritchie, W. *The Authenticity of the Rhesus of Euripides.* Cambridge: Cambridge University Press, 1964.

Rosenmeyer, Thomas. G. *The Masks of Tragedy.* Austin: The University of Texas, 1963.

Seaford, Richard. *Euripides: Cyclops.* Oxford: Oxford University Press, 1984.

_____. *Reciprocity and Ritual; Homer and Tragedy in the Developing City State*. Oxford: Oxford University Press, 1994.

_____. *Euripides: Bacchae*. Warminster, UK: Aris and Phillips, 1996.

Segal, Charles. "The Tragedy of the *Hippolytus*: The Waters of Ocean and the Untouched Meadow." *Harvard Studies in Classical Philology* 70 1965.

_____. "Shame and Purity in Euripides' *Hippolytus*." *Hermes* 98, 1970.

_____. *Interpreting Greek Tragedy: Myth, Poetry, Text*. Ithaca, N.Y.: Cornell University Press, 1986.

_____. *Euripides and the Poetics of Sorrow*. Durham, N.C.: Duke University Press, 1993.

_____. *Dionysiac Poetics and Euripides'* Bacchae. Expanded ed. Princeton: Princeton University Press, 1997.

Segal, C. P. "The Two Worlds of Euripides' *Helen*." *Transactions of the American Philological Association* 102, 1971.

Segal, Erich, ed. *Euripides: A Collection of Critical Essays*. Englewood Cliffs, N.J.: Prentice-Hall, 1968.

_____. *Oxford Essays in Greek Tragedy*. Oxford: Oxford University Press, 1984.

Slater, Philip. *The Glory of Hera*. Boston: Beacon Press, 1968.

Smith, W. "The Ironic Structure in *Alcestis*." *Phoenix* 14, 1960.

Smyth, Herbert Weir. *Aeschylus*. 2 vols. Cambridge, Mass.: Harvard University Press, 1963.

Sourvinou-Inwood, Christine. *Reading Greek Culture: Texts and Images, Rituals and Myths*. Oxford: Oxford University Press, 1991.

Steiner, George. *The Death of Tragedy*. New York: Alfred A. Knopf, 1961.

Stevens, P. T. *Euripides: Andromache*. Oxford: Oxford University Press, 1971.

Strohm, Hans. *Euripides*. Munich: Beck, 1957.

Taplin, Oliver. *Greek Tragedy in Action*. Berkeley and Los Angeles: The University of California Press; London: Methuen, 1978.

_____. *Comic Angels and Other Approaches to Greek Drama Through Vase-Paintings*. Oxford: Oxford University Press, 1993.

Turner, Victor. *The Forest of Symbols*. Ithaca, N.Y.: Cornell University Press, 1973.

_____, *Dramas, Fields, and Metaphors*. Ithaca, N.Y.: Cornell University Press, 1974.

Turyn, A. *The Byzantine Manuscript Tradition of the Plays of Euripides.* Urbana: University of Illinois Press, 1957

Verrall, A. W. *Essays on Four Plays of Euripides.* Cambridge: Cambridge University Press, 1905.

Vernant, Jean-Pierre, and Pierre Vidal-Naquet, eds. *Myth and Tragedy in Ancient Greece.* New York: Zone Books, 1990.

Vernant, J. P. *Myth and Thought Among the Greeks.* London and Boston: Routledge and Kegan Paul, 1983.

_____. *Myth and Society in Ancient Greece.* New York: Zone Books, 1990.

Vickers, Brian. *Towards Greek Tragedy.* London: Longman, 1973.

Webster, T .B. L. *The Tragedies of Euripides.* London: Methuen, 1967.

West, M. L. *Euripides: Orestes.* Warminster, UK: Aris and Phillips, 1987.

Whitman, Cedric H. *Euripides and the Full Circle of Myth.* Cambridge, Mass.: Harvard University Press, 1974.

Wilkins, J. *Euripides: Children of Heracles.* Oxford: Oxford University Press, 1993.

Willink, C. W. *Euripides: Orestes.* Oxford: Oxford University Press, 1986.

Wilson, J. R., ed. *Twentieth-Century Interpretations of Euripides' Alcestis.* Englewood Cliffs, N.J.: Prentice-Hall, 1968.

Winkler, John. *The Constraints of Desire: The Anthropology of Sex and Gender in Ancient Greece.* New York and London: Routledge, 1990.

Winkler, John J., and Froma I. Zeitlin, eds. *Nothing to Do With Dionysos? Athenian Drama in Its Social Context.* Princeton: Princeton University Press, 1992.

Winnington-Ingram, R. P. *Euripides and Dionysus: An Interpretation of the Bacchae.* Cambridge, Mass.: Harvard University Press, 1948.

Zeitlin, Froma I. *Playing the Other: Gender and Society in Classical Greek Literature.* Chicago: University of Chicago Press, 1996.

Zuntz, G. "Is the *Heraclidae* Mutilated?" *Classical Quarterly* 41, 1947.

_____. *The Political Plays of Euripides.* Manchester: Manchester University Press, 1963.

_____. *An Inquiry into the Transmission of the Plays of Euripides.* Cambridge: Cambridge University Press, 1965.

THEATERS, PRODUCERS

Else, Gerald F. *The Origin and Early Form of Greek Tragedy.* Martin Classical Lectures, vol. 20. Cambridge: Harvard University Press, 1965.

Fergusson, Francis. *The Idea of Theater: A Study of Ten Plays, The Art of Drama in Changing Perspective.* Princeton, N.J.: Princeton University Press; London: Oxford University Press, 1949.

Garkand, Robert. *The Greek Way of Life.* Ithaca, N.Y.: Cornell University Press, 1990.

Neils, Jenifer. *Goddess and Polis: The Panathenaic Festival in Ancient Athens.* Princeton. N.J.: Princeton University Press, 1992.

Parke, H. W. *Festivals of the Athenians.* Ithaca, N.Y.: Cornell University Press, 1977.

Pickard-Cambridge, A. W. *The Theatre of Dionysus in Athens.* Oxford: The Clarendon Press, 1968.

_____. *Dithyramb, Tragedy and Comedy.* Revised ed. Oxford: Oxford University Press, 1988.

_____. *The Dramatic Festivals of Athens.* Oxford: The Clarendon Press, 1988.

Roberts, Patrick. *The Psychology of Tragic Drama.* Boston and London: Routledge and Kegan Paul, 1975.

ACTORS, DIRECTORS, THEATER PROFESSIONALS

Arnott, Peter. *Greek Scenic Conventions in the Fifth Century B.C.* Oxford: Oxford University Press, 1962.

_____. *Public and Performance in the Greek Theatre.* London: Routledge, 1989.

Bain, David. *Actors and Audience: A Study of Asides and Related Conventions in Greek Drama.* Oxford: Oxford University Press, 1977.

_____. *Masters, Servants, and Orders in Greek Tragedy: Some Aspects of Dramatic Technique and Convention.* Manchester, UK: Manchester University Press, 1981.

Bartsch, S. *Actors in the Audience.* Cambridge, Mass.: Harvard University Press, 1994.

Gebhard, Elizabeth. "The Form of the orchestra in the Early Greek Theatre." *Hesperia* 43 (1974).

Georgiades, Thrasybulos. *Greek Music, Verse and Dance.* New York: Da Capo Press, 1973.

Green, J. R., and E. Handley. *Images of the Greek Theatre.* Austin: University of Texas Press, 1995

Hammond, N. G. L. "The Conditions of Dramatic Production to the Death of Aeschylus." *Greek, Roman and Byzantine Studies* 13 (1972).

Hornby, Richard. *Script into Performance.* Austin: University of Texas Press, 1977.

Kernodle, George R. "Symbolic Action in the Greek Choral Odes?" *Classical Journal* 53 (1957/8).

Kitto, H. D. F. "The Dance in Greek Tragedy." *Journal of Hellenistic Studies* 75 (1955).

Ley, Graham, and Michael Ewans. "The Orchestra as Acting Area in Greek Tragedy." *Ramus* 14 (1985).

Lonsdale, Stephen H. *Dance and Ritual Play in Greek Religion.* Baltimore, Md.: The Johns Hopkins University Press, 1993.

Rehm, Rush. "The Staging of Suppliant Plays." *Greek, Roman and Byzantine Studies* 29 (1988).

_____. *The Greek Tragic Theatre.* London and New York: Routledge, 1992.

Sutton, D. F. *The Greek Satyr Play.* Meisenheim am Glan: Hain, 1980.

Vellacott, Philip. *Ironic Drama: A Study of Euripides' Method and Meaning.* Cambridge: Cambridge University Press, 1975.

_____. *The Greek Sense of Theatre: Tragedy Reviewed.* London and New York: Methuen, 1984.

Walton, J. Michael. *Greek Theatre Practice.* Westport, Conn., and London: Greenwood Press, 1980.

Wiles, David. *Tragedy in Athens.* Cambridge and New York: Cambridge University Press, 1997.

THE EDITIONS OF EURIPIDES' WORKS USED FOR THIS BOOK

Euripides. *The Complete Plays.* Vol. I. Translated by Carl R. Mueller. Lyme, N.H.: Smith and Kraus, 2005.

_____. *The Complete Plays.* Vol. II. Translated by Carl R. Mueller. Lyme, N.H.: Smith and Kraus, 2005.

_____. *The Complete Plays.* Vol. III. Translated by Carl R. Mueller. Lyme, N.H.: Smith and Kraus, 2005.

_____. *The Complete Plays.* Vol. IV. Translated by Carl R. Mueller. Lyme, N.H.: Smith and Kraus, 2005.

SOURCES CITED IN THIS BOOK

Kovacs, David. "Euripides *Hippolytus* 100 and the Meaning of the Prologue." *Classical Philology* 75, 1980.

_____. "Where Is Aegisthus' Head?" *Classical Philology* 35, 1985.

_____. *The Heroic Muse: Studies in the* Hippolytus *and* Hecuba *of Euripides.* Baltimore, Md.: The Johns Hopkins University Press, 1987.

Easterling, P. E. "The Infanticide in Euripides' *Medea.*" *Yale Classical Studies* 25, 1977.

_____, ed. *The Cambridge Companion to Greek Tragedy.* Cambridge: Cambridge University Press, 1997.

Thucydides. *The Peloponnesian Wars.* Rex Warner, tr. Harmondsworth, UK: Penguin Classics, 1972.

Awards

"And the winner is . . . "

YEAR BC	DIONYSIA FESTIVAL IN ATHENS	LENAEA FESTIVAL IN ATHENS
ca 534	Thespis *Unknown title*	
484	Aeschylus *Unknown title*	
476	Phrynichus *Phoenissae*	
468	Sophocles *Triptolemus*	
ca 467	Aeschylus *Seven Against Thebes*	
ca 463	Aeschylus *Danaid trilogy*	
ca 459	Aeschylus *Suppliant Women*	
ca 458	Aeschylus *Oresteia*	
455	**Euripides** ***Daughters of Pelias*** (third prize)	
447	Sophocles *Unknown title*	
442	A prize is institutionalized and first awarded to the best comic actor at the City Dionysia. (unknown recipient)	
441	**Euripides** ***Unknown title***	
ca 439	Sophocles *Unknown title* (first prize) **Euripides** ***Alcestis*** (second prize)	
431	Euphorion (son of Aeschylus) *Unknown title* (first prize) Sophocles *Unknown title* (second prize) **Euripides** ***Medea, Philoctetes, Dictys, Theristae*** (third prize)	

428	Euripides *Hippolytus*	
427		Aristophanes *Banqueters* (second prize)
426	Aristophanes *Babylonians*	
425		Aristophanes *Acharnians*
424		Aristophanes *Knights*
423	Aristophanes *Clouds I* (third prize out of three)	
422		Aristophanes *Proagon* (first prize) Aristophanes *Wasps* (second prize)
421	Aristophanes *Peace I* (second prize)	
415	Xenocles *Oedipus, Lycaun, Bacchae,* *Athamas* (first prize) **Euripides** *Trojan Women, Alexandrus, Palamedes, Sisyphus* (second prize)	
414	Aristophanes *Birds* (second prize)	
410	**Euripides** ***Phoenician Women*** (second prize)	
409	Sophocles *Philoctetes*	
ca 405	**Euripides** ***Bacchae*** **(posthumously produced)**	Aristophanes *Frogs*
401	Sophocles *Oedipus at Colonus* (posthumously produced)	
387	Aristophanes *Cocolus*	
321	Menander *Anger*	

Unknown title = play lost

First prize unless otherwise specified

Aristophanes won prizes in the comedy genre; the others won in the tragedy genre.

INDEX

The entries in the index include highlights from the main In an Hour essay portion of the book.

ABOUT THE AUTHOR

Carl Mueller was a professor in the Department of Theater at the University of California, Los Angeles, from 1967 until his death in 2008. There he directed and taught theater history, criticism, dramatic literature, and playwriting. He was educated at Northwestern University, where he received a B.S. in English. After work in graduate English at the University of California, Berkeley, he received his M.A. in Playwriting at UCLA, where he also completed his Ph.D. in Theater History and Criticism. In 1960–1961 he was a Fulbright Scholar in Berlin.

A translator for more than forty years, he translated and published works by Büchner, Brecht, Wedekind, Hauptmann, Hofmannsthal, and Hebbel, to name a few. His published translation of von Horváth's *Tales from the Vienna Woods* was given its London West End premiere in July 1999. For Smith and Kraus he translated individual volumes of plays by Schnitzler, Strindberg, Pirandello, Kleist, and Wedekind. His translation of Goethe's *Faust* Part One and Part Two appeared in 2004. He also translated for Smith and Kraus *Sophokles: The Complete Plays* (2000), a two-volume *Aeschylus: The Complete Plays* (2002), and a four-volume *Euripides: The Complete Plays* (2005). His translations have been performed in every English-speaking country and have appeared on BBC-TV.

Smith and Kraus wishes to acknowledge Dr. Susan Ford Wiltshire, Professor of Classics, Emerita, Vanderbilt University. She was immensely helpful with the spellings of Greek names and places.

We thank Hugh Denard, whose enlightened permissions policy reflects an understanding that copyright law is intended to both protect the rights of creators of intellectual property as well as to encourage its use for the public good.

Know the playwright, love the play.

Open a new door to theater study, performance, and audience satisfaction with these Playwrights In an Hour titles.

ANCIENT GREEK

Aeschylus   Aristophanes   Euripides   Sophocles

RENAISSANCE

William Shakespeare

MODERN

Anton Chekhov   Noël Coward   Lorraine Hansberry
Henrik Ibsen   Arthur Miller   Molière   Eugene O'Neill
Arthur Schnitzler   George Bernard Shaw   August Strindberg
Frank Wedekind   Oscar Wilde   Thornton Wilder
Tennessee Williams

CONTEMPORARY

Edward Albee   Alan Ayckbourn   Samuel Beckett
Theresa Rebeck   Sarah Ruhl   Sam Shepard   Tom Stoppard
August Wilson

To purchase or for more information
visit our web site inanhourbooks.com